The Right Joke
For The
Right Occasion

The Right Joke For The Right Occasion

by

Kevin Goldstein-Jackson

PAPERFRONTS

ELLIOT RIGHT WAY BOOKS
KINGSWOOD, SURREY, U.K.

Printed and bound in Great Britain by
Cox & Wyman Ltd, Reading

Contents

Dedication

This book is dedicated to myself for being such a genius to write it. I already take a bow every time I look in a mirror – but it's nice to be recognized in print, too. I have *not* dedicated this book to my parents as I already send them a letter of congratulations every year – on my birthday. This remarkable volume is also dedicated to Debbie Ng for being so polite when I tell jokes – she covers her mouth when she yawns. She's the only woman I know who is like wine – she improves with age. And, more seriously, this book is dedicated to her in the hope that as she gets older her voice will change – from 'No' to 'Yes'.

Introduction

As I sit in my tiny writer's room – it's so small even the mice are hunchbacks – I can now look back on the years, months, days, – well, two or three hours anyway, that went into the writing and compiling of *The Right Joke for the Right Occasion*.

There are over 600 jokes, listed alphabetically under subject, and the Directory to the Book, which starts on page 9, provides instant reference to jokes covering hundreds of different subjects.

It covers even the most peculiar subjects, so that, should anyone have occasion to address a meeting of cannibals or Martians for example, at least he or she can find one or two suitable jokes to tell them.

To encourage you to read it, the work also includes subjects like 'Population Explosion', 'Hypochondriac' and even 'Lumberjack'.

I don't claim to have written all the jokes in this book – but merely dredged them up from the dark remembering recesses of my brain, with a goodly number of them being my own, original work – if it is possible to claim any jokes as being 'original'.

Incidentally, I have also written this book fairly slowly, to help those who are not quick readers.

But I hope, after reading *The Right Joke for the Right Occasion*, you will not think of it in the same way as the girl who asked 'Do you know what good clean fun is?' to which her boyfriend replied 'No, what good is it?'

K.G-J.

Directory to the Book

If you are just reading the book for fun, skip the next 9 pages because the actual jokes don't start till page 19

This section is for the person who has to make a speech, or who needs a joke on a particular subject. In the directory, the numbers shown are the joke numbers, not page numbers.

Remember that the secrets of being a good jokeman lie as much in the way you tell it as in the joke itself. Be enthusiastic, watch the 'timing' of the 'punch line'. Never tell a joke which does not suit the company. In conversation, try to tell jokes which 'arise' from the subject being discussed. There are over 600 jokes in the book, which should be enough to keep you going for several minutes!

10

Pornography: *Joke no.* 415
Professor: *Joke no.* 416, 417
Protester's Placards: *Joke no.* 418, 419, 420
Psychiatrist: *Joke no.* 421, 422, 423

Quack Doctor: *Joke no.* 424
Questions: *Joke no.* 425, 426, 427, 428, 429, 430, 431, 432,
433, 434, 435, 436, 437, 438, 439, 440, 441, 442, 443, 444,
445, 446, 447, 448, 449, 450, 451, 452, 453, 454, 455, 456,
457, 458, 459, 460, 461, 462, 463, 464, 465, 466, 467, 468,
469, 470, 471, 472, 473
Quick Quips: *Joke no.* 2, 5, 6, 7, 8, 14, 15, 16, 18, 19, 20, 21,
22, 26, 27, 28, 29, 30, 31, 32, 33, 34, 35, 36, 37, 38, 40, 41,
42, 43, 45, 47, 51, 53, 58, 60, 66, 67, 68, 69, 70, 71, 73, 75,
76, 77, 79, 80, 81, 82, 83, 84, 85, 86, 87, 88, 89, 92, 95,
96, 97, 98, 99, 100, 103, 138, 141, 142, 144, 147, 149,
150, 152, 153, 157, 158, 159, 160, 161, 163, 164, 165, 166,
167, 170, 171, 172, 173, 176, 180, 182, 183, 184, 186, 188,
205, 206, 215, 220, 223, 224, 227, 228, 229, 230, 238, 240,
244, 245, 251, 252, 253, 254, 255, 260, 263, 265, 268, 270,
271, 272, 273, 274, 276, 277, 278, 279, 280, 284, 286, 287,
288, 289, 290, 291, 297, 298, 299, 300, 301, 302, 303, 304,
305, 306, 307, 308, 309, 310, 311, 312, 313, 314, 315, 316,
317, 318, 319, 320, 321, 323, 324, 325, 326, 327, 329, 330,
333, 335, 336, 340, 341, 345, 347, 348, 355, 357, 360, 364,
367, 369, 375, 376, 377, 378, 379, 380, 381, 382, 383, 384,
385, 386, 387, 388, 389, 391, 394, 395, 396, 401, 405, 406,
407, 413, 414, 418, 419, 420, 421, 422, 423, 425, 426, 428,
429, 430, 431, 432, 433, 434, 435, 436, 437, 438, 439, 440,
441, 442, 443, 444, 445, 447, 448, 449, 450, 451, 452, 453,
454, 455, 456, 457, 458, 459, 460, 461, 462, 463, 465, 466,
467, 468, 469, 470, 471, 472, 473, 474, 479, 480, 482, 483,
484, 485, 486, 487, 492, 497, 498, 499, 500, 501, 502, 503,
505, 506, 507, 508, 509, 510, 511, 512, 513, 521, 524, 525,
526, 527, 528, 529, 530, 532, 534, 538, 541, 546, 548, 553,
556, 557, 561, 562, 564, 565, 571, 572, 579, 580, 582, 583,

14

584, 592, 593, 594, 595, 596, 597, 598, 603, 604, 607, 609,
612, 615

Rabbits: *Joke no.* 474
Racing: *Joke no.* 475, 476, 477
Rats: *Joke no.* 478
Red Corpuscles: *Joke no.* 479
Reincarnation: *Joke no.* 480
Religious: *Joke no.* 1, 10, 22, 23, 24, 177, 204, 206, 208, 209,
214, 221, 376, 569, 587, 588, 589, 590, 591, 592
Rhinoceros: *Joke no.* 481
Romance: *Joke no.* 73, 95, 370, 371, 482, 483, 484, 485, 486,
487, 488, 489, 490, 491, 492, 493, 494, 495, 496, 497, 498,
499, 500, 501, 502, 503, 504, 505, 506, 507, 508, 509, 510,
511

Sadist: *Joke no.* 512, 513
Salvation Army: *Joke no.* 514
School: *Joke no.* 515, 516, 517, 518, 519, 520, 521, 522, 523
School Report: *Joke no.* 524, 525, 526, 527, 528, 529
Scottish Flavour: *Joke no.* 342, 369, 530, 531, 532, 533
Sea: *Joke no.* 249, 470, 534
Seance: *Joke no.* 535
Servants: *Joke no.* 185, 536, 537
Sexy Stories: *Joke no.* 12, 13, 25, 71, 73, 81, 83, 88, 240, 356,
357, 358, 361, 362, 366, 371, 395, 413, 414, 474, 476, 477,
479, 482, 483, 485, 492, 493, 494, 495, 496, 498, 500, 502,
504, 505, 506, 510, 514, 519, 538, 539, 540, 541, 542, 543,
547, 577, 578, 582, 592, 602
Shipwrecked Sailor: *Joke no.* 544
Shoes: *Joke no.* 545
Sin: *Joke no.* 546, 547, 548
Speeches: *Joke no.* 549, 550
Spiders: *Joke no.* 147
Spies: *Joke no.* 551, 552

JOKES

A

ACCIDENT
1. A man rushed into a pub in a rather agitated state. 'Does anyone here own a large black cat with a white collar?' he asked, somewhat nervously. There was no reply.

'Does anybody own a large black cat with a white collar?' asked the man again, raising his voice even higher above the general noise of the bar. But still no one answered his question.

'Oh dear,' muttered the man. 'I must have run over the vicar.'

ACOUSTICS
2. 'The acoustics in this theatre are fantastic.'
   'Pardon?'

ACTING
3. Timothy desperately wanted to be a famous actor and always believed in trying to 'live' any parts he was asked to play. When he was invited to audition for the part of Abraham Lincoln in a new play, Timothy read all about Lincoln. He researched Lincoln's background for weeks and then dressed to look exactly like him – black hat, black cloak, red sash and large black boots. After admiring himself in a mirror he set off for the audition. He didn't get the part – but on the way home he was assassinated.

ADVERTISEMENTS
4. Worktex bras – the largest manufacturers of bras in the world. We have a hand in nine out of ten bras in Britain.

5. Midget seeks work – preferably as a stunt man.

6. Do you suffer from Dan Druff? Well, tell him to go away.

7. For sale: two single beds and a worn carpet.

8. Lavatory cleaner wanted to work on chain gang. Could you do this job? Some people are a flushing success at it.

9. Little girl: 'Mummy, why are your hands so soft?'

Mother: 'Because I always use Pixie Solid for washing my dishes.'

Little girl: 'But why does it get your hands so soft?'

Mother: 'Because the money Pixie Solid pay me for this commercial enables me to buy an automatic dish washer.'

10. The tea manufacturers wanted a new advertising gimmick, so the senior creative man at their advertising agency decided to go to Rome to see if he could persuade the Pope to make a TV commercial.

The Pope gave the adman an audience and he made his request. 'We'll give you one hundred thousand pounds for a ten second commercial. All you have to do is say: "Give us this day our daily tea".'

'I'm sorry,' replied the Pope, 'but I cannot do as you request.'

'Five hundred thousand,' offered the adman.

'I'm afraid not,' said the Pope, solemnly.

'All right. One million pounds. And that's our very last offer.'

But still the Pope refused to make the commercial and the adman left. On the way home the adman turned to his secretary and said: 'That's odd. I mean, the Pope refusing to do a commercial for tea. I wonder how much the bread people are giving him.'

AIR HOSTESS

11. The air hostess was being interviewed by her boss. 'Tell me, what would you do if you found yourself in a shallow dive?'

Air hostess: 'I'd drink up quickly and get out.'

ARTIFICIAL INSEMINATION

12. All the farmers in the area were going over to artificial insemination for their herds – all, that is, except Walter Manglewurzel. Walter refused to have anything to do with such new-fangled ideas, but one day the vet decided to convince him of the advantages of artificial insemination for his herd of cows.

Well, Walter stopped harnessing his wife to the plough to listen to the vet, and he was pleased with what he heard and agreed to give the idea a try.

That afternoon, the vet returned and said: 'Did you put the bucket of hot water and a towel in the cowsheds like I asked?'

'Yes,' replied Walter. 'And there's a hook behind the door you can hang your trousers on.'

B

BABIES

13. There were two babies in the pram. One baby turned to the other baby and said: 'Are you a little girl or a little boy?'

'I don't know,' was the giggled reply.

'I can tell,' said the first baby gleefully, and he dived beneath the bedclothes and then resurfaced. 'You're a girl and I'm a boy,' he announced proudly.

'That was clever,' said the baby girl. 'How could you tell?'

'Easy! You've got pink bootees and I've got blue ones.'

14. 'But Henry, it isn't our baby.'

'Shut up – it's a better pram.'

15. Woman, peering into a pram: 'Isn't your baby small?'

Mother: 'Well, I have only been married three months.'

BANKING

16. Customer: 'And how do I stand for a £5,000 loan?'

Bank manager: 'You don't – you grovel.'

17. A young woman went into a bank and asked to withdraw some money.

'Can you identify yourself?' asked the bank clerk.

The young woman opened her handbag, took out a mirror, looked into it and said: 'Yes, it's me all right.'

BARBERS

18. Barber: 'Were you wearing a red scarf when you came in?'

Customer: 'No.'

Barber: 'Oh! Then I must have cut your throat.'

19. Barbers always seem to make cutting remarks.

BEES

20. Why do bees hum? Because they don't know the words.

BELCH

21. 'How dare you belch in front of my wife!'
   'Why – was it her turn?'

BIBLICAL

22. Eve was so jealous of Adam that when he came home each night she used to count his ribs.

23. When God had finally formulated his Ten Commandments he approached all the various races and tribes of people on the Earth and asked if they would like his Commandments.

The Arabs were rather cautious and asked: 'What do these Commandments say?'

'Well,' said God, 'one of them says: "Thou shalt not steal." '

'But that's no good,' replied the Arabs. 'We can't possibly take them as we earn much of our living by plundering travellers.'

God then asked the French if they would take his Commandments, but they, too, wanted to know what they commanded. When God got to 'Thou shalt not commit adultery,' the French stopped Him, shaking their heads sadly. 'We do not think these Commandments – especially that one – are suitable for us.'

God offered his Commandments to many other peoples, but they all rejected them as being unsuitable to their particular way of life. Eventually, in desperation, God approached the Jews.

'How much do they cost?' asked Moses.

'They are completely free of charge,' replied God.

'Good,' said Moses. 'In that case, we'll take them all – and can we have two sets as well?'

24. It may interest many travellers to know that British Rail is mentioned in the Book of Genesis. It states that God created every creeping thing.

BOASTING
25. A young man was loudly lamenting to everyone in the bar that his doctor had ordered him to give up half his sex life.

'Which half are you going to give up?' asked a bored listener. 'Talking about it – or thinking about it?'

BOOKS
26. HOW TO MAKE AN IGLOO by S. K. Mow.
27. HOW TO MAKE SOLID MEALS by C. Ment.
28. NO FOOD by M. T. Cupboard.
29. THE ART OF STRIPTEASE by Eva Drawsoff.
30. HORSE RIDING COMPETITIONS by Jim Karna.
31. HOME HAIRCUTTING by Shaun Hedd.
32. NECK EXERCISES by G. Rarff.
33. OUTSIZE CLOTHES by L. E. Fant.
34. DO IT YOURSELF BRAIN SURGERY by Drs. Out & I. Malone.

BUDGERIGARS
35. What do you call a constipated budgie? Chirrup of figs.
36. What do you call a budgie run over by a lawn mower? Shredded tweet.
37. What do you call a nine foot budgie? Sir.
38. Where does a nine foot budgie sleep? Anywhere it wants to.

BUILDERS
39. Three lunatics were working on a building site, sup-

posedly digging a trench. After a few hours the foreman came along and was surprised to find one of the men digging furiously while the other two were standing motionless, their shovels in the air, and claiming that they were both lamp posts. The foreman sacked the two men immediately and told them to go home. But the man in the trench also stopped work.

'It's all right,' said the foreman. 'I haven't fired you. You were working very well, so carry on.'

'How,' asked the man, 'do you expect me to work in the dark?'

BUTCHERS

40. Woman: 'I want a nice piece of bacon. And make it lean.'

Butcher: 'Which way, madam?'

C

CABBAGES
41. There were two parallel lines of cabbages, so the farmer called it a dual cabbage way.

CAMEL
42. What do you call a camel with three humps? Humphrey.

43. Then there was the Arab who was so fat his camel had its hump underneath.

CANNIBAL
44. The cannibal drank a lot of soup out of an enormous cooking pot, then turned to his friend, belched, and said: 'I've had a bellyfull of your mother.'

45. A Jewish cannibal was very successful in the heart of the jungle when he set up a crematorium and sold instant people.

46. 'Do you like beans?'
   'Yes, very much.'
   'What sort do you like eating best?'
   'Human bein's.'

47. What do cannibals eat for breakfast? Buttered host.

48. The cannibal came home to find his wife chopping up snakes and a very small man. 'Oh no!' he groaned. 'Not snake an pygmy pie again!'

49. As one cannibal said to the other, tasting the stew: 'It contains health giving vitamin Bill Brown.'

CARPENTRY
50. How can you easily decide whether to use a screw or a nail when doing carpentry? Drive in a nail – if the wood splits, you should have used a screw.

CARS

51. I recently bought a baby car – it doesn't go anywhere without a rattle.

52. Henry was trying to sell his battered old car for £500. His friend, Tom, said he would pay 10% less than the price Henry was asking for the car. But Henry was not very good at figures so he said he would think about Tom's offer. That evening, when he was in his usual bar, Henry asked the barmaid: 'If I offered you £500 less 10% what would you take off?'

The barmaid hesitated slightly, then replied: 'Everything except my ear-rings.'

53. I've got a two-tone car – black and rust.

CATS

54. The vet had just supervised the delivery of a litter of kittens to the old spinster's cat. 'I just don't know how it could have happened,' said the spinster. 'Tibbles is never allowed out and no other cats are ever allowed into the house.'

'But what about him?' asked the vet, pointing to a large tom cat sitting in an armchair.

'Oh, don't be silly,' replied the spinster. 'That's her brother.'

CHEMIST

55. Customer: 'Chemist, I'd like some poison for mice.'

Chemist: 'Have you tried Boots?'

Customer: 'I want to poison them – not kick them to death.'

CHINESE WAITER

56. Chinese waiter! There's a dead fly in my bird's nest soup.'

'Well, for two cents what do you expect – dead eagle?'

57. 'Chinese waiter! What is this stuff in the bowl?'

'It's bean soup, sir.'

'I don't want to know what it's been – what is it now?'

CINEMA

58. Young girl in a cinema: 'Take your hand off my knee! No, not you, *you!*'

59. The man in the front seat of the cinema was making groaning noises very loudly during a tender love scene on the screen.

'Shut up!' hissed the audience around him, but still the man continued making horrible noises.

Eventually, the manager was called and he marched down the aisle until he came to the noisy man. 'Get up!' demanded the manager.

'Ooooooh! Aaaaaaaargh!' shouted the man, in reply.

'Where are you from?' asked the manager.

'F ... Fr ...' groaned the man '... from th ... the balcony.'

60. Dracula films are fangtastic.

61. The young girl was complaining to one of her friends. 'It was terrible! I had to change my seat five times at the cinema last night.'

'Why?' asked the friend. 'Did some chap bother you?'

'Yes – eventually.'

CLOAKROOM ATTENDANT

62. The theatre's cloakroom attendant was obviously very new to her job, and the man watched in silent amusement while she struggled to find his coat. She knocked clothes off their hangers and became more and more flustered when she could not trace the man's coat.

After nearly fifteen minutes of searching, a long queue had built up behind the man and his air of quiet amusement had given way to anger. Eventually he muttered: 'Don't bother to continue looking for my coat – I'll go without it.

Perhaps if I come back tomorrow you might have found it. Although that seems most unlikely as you're the most incompetent person I've ever had the misfortune to meet!'

As he began to make his way out of the theatre the cloakroom attendant called: 'You mean old man! What about my tip?'

CLOCK
63. The German could not get his clock to work properly. No matter what he did with it – shake it, take the back off it, blow on it – the clock insisted on only going 'tick'. Finally, his patience at an end, the German held up the clock in front of him and hissed: 'Ve haf vays of making you tock.'

CONVERSATIONS
64. 'Why are you in such a hurry?'
'I'm on my way to the doctor – I don't like the look of my wife.'
'Oh! Then I'll come with you – I hate the sight of mine, too.'

65. 'My wife speaks through her nose.'
'Why?'
'She's worn her mouth out.'

66. 'Do you come here often?'
'I'm your wife, stupid!'

67. 'Measles.'
'That's a rash thing to say.'

68. 'I had to give up tap dancing.'
'Why?'
'I kept falling in the sink.'

69. 'That's a nice suit you're wearing – who went for the fitting?'

70. 'I didn't come here to be insulted.'
'Why – where do you normally go?'

71. 'Did he have a weakness for ladies?'
'No – a great strength.'

72. 'Boy, you should have seen the stripper at the Club last night. That unbelievable 55-26-37 figure . . .'
'What kind of a dance did she do?'
'Well, she didn't actually dance – it was more like she crawled around on stage and tried to stand up.'

73. 'Do you ever talk to your wife when making love?'
'Only if she telephones.'

74. "What's the difference between a postbox and an elephant?'
'I don't know.'
'Well, I'm not giving you any letters to post.'

75. 'Excuse me, can you tell me the time?'
'I'm sorry, but I'm a stranger here myself.'

76. 'I say! Look over there – isn't that Hortense?'
'No – she looks quite relaxed to me.'

77. 'I don't know what to make of him.'
'What about a standard lamp.'

78. 'How did you get that puncture?'
'Ran over a milk bottle.'
'But why didn't you see it?'
'Because a stupid kid had it under his coat.'

79. 'Why are you so angry?'
'Because it's all the rage.'

80. 'My mother made me a homosexual.'
'If I sent her the wool, would she make me one too?'

81. 'Do you smoke after making love?'
'I don't know, I've never looked.'

82. 'Understand you buried your wife last week?'
'Had to . . . dead, you know.'

83. 'What are you doing in the cellar, children?'
'Making love.'
'That's nice, dears. Don't fight.'

84. 'Mummy, there's a man with a bill at the door.'
'Don't be silly, dear. It must be a duck with a hat on.'

85. 'I'm going to hypnotize you.'
'What makes you think I'm Jewish?'

86. 'Well, how do you find yourself these cold, winter mornings?'
'Oh, I just throw back the blankets and there I am.'

87. 'Will the band play anything I request?'
'Certainly, sir.'
'Then tell them to play dominoes.'

88. 'What do virgins eat for breakfast?'
'I don't know.'
'Huh! Just as I thought.'

COW
89. The first time the little girl from the big city ever saw a cow she thought it was a bull that had swallowed a glove.

COWBOY
90. 'Who painted my horse blue?' yelled the angry cowboy, entering the saloon.

Everyone was silent, and then a massive cowboy stood up and admitted to having done the deed. As he looked up at the huge man towering over him the newcomer said softly: 'Oh! I only wanted to know when you're going to give it a second coat.'

91. The Lone Ranger and Tonto were riding along one morning when suddenly they saw five hundred Sioux chasing up behind them. Galloping ahead as fast as they could they were astonished to find another five hundred Indians – this time Apaches – racing towards them from the front, all dressed in war paint and giving excited war whoops.

The lone Ranger slowed his horse to a gentle trot and turned to Tonto and said: 'Well, old friend, it looks as if this is going to be the finish for both of us.'

Tonto shook his head sadly, and said: 'What do you mean, *both* of us – White Man?'

92. 'This town isn't big enough for both of us.'

'O.K. Let's go on a diet.'

'What colour?'

93. Two men in a saloon were playing cards. One of them thumped the table happily with his fist and cried: 'I win!'

'What have you got?' asked the other cowboy.

'Four aces.'

'I'm afraid you don't win.'

'That's almost impossible,' declared the first man. 'What cards have you got?'

'Two nines and a loaded gun.'

'Oh,' said the first man. 'You win. But how come you're so lucky?'

D

DECEIT
94. In the divorce court the judge frowned and said: 'So, Miss Brown, you admit that you stayed in a hotel with this man?'

Woman: 'Yes, I do. But I couldn't help it. He deceived me.'

Judge: 'Really? How?'

Woman: 'Well, he told the reception clerk I was his wife.'

DEFINITIONS
95. Cloak: mating call of a Chinese frog.

96. Eunuch: man cut out to be a bachelor.

97. Blunderbuss: a coach load of spinsters on their way to a maternity hospital.

98. Vice versa: dirty poems.

99. Mistress: something between a mister and a mattress.

100. Mushroom: place where Eskimos train their dogs.

DENTIST
101. Man: 'Give it me straight – how am I?'

Dentist: 'Well, sir your teeth are all right – but I'm afraid your gums will have to come out.'

DIETING
102. At a recent lecture entitled 'How To Lose Weight Easily,' Mrs. Emily Plum told the amazing story of how she lost over eighteen pounds in five minutes. Said this remarkable lady: 'I just cut off a leg.'

DIVING
103. A diver working 300 feet below the surface of the Eng-

lish Channel got a message from his ship saying: 'Come up quick! We're sinking.'

DOCKER

104. 'Have you been working in these docks all your life?' asked the new TV reporter.

'Not yet,' replied the docker.

105. A London docker was walking along, kicking a tortoise. A policeman watched this for a few minutes, then went up to the docker and asked: 'Why are you kicking this poor defenceless tortoise?'

The docker paused slightly, then replied: 'Because it's been following me around all day.'

DOCTOR

106. Receptionist: 'Dr. Wynazonski is waiting for you.'
   Patient: 'Which doctor?'
   Receptionist: 'Oh, no, he's fully qualified.'

107. Student doctor: 'Please sir, there's some writing on this patient's foot.'
   Famous surgeon: 'Ah, yes! That's a footnote.'

108. Patient: 'Doctor, how can I live to be a hundred?'
   Doctor: 'Well, I suggest you give up eating rich food and going out with women.'
   Patient: 'And then will I live to be a hundred?'
   Doctor: 'No – but it will seem like it.'

109. Patient: 'Doctor, my hair keeps falling out. Have you got anything to keep it in?'
   Doctor: 'What about a cardboard box?'

110. Patient: 'Doctor, have you got anything for my liver?'
   Doctor: 'What about some onions?'

111. Patient: 'Doctor, sorry to trouble you again, but what can you give me for flat feet?'
   Doctor: 'What about a bicycle pump?'

112. Receptionist: 'The doctor is so funny he'll soon have you in stitches.'
Patient: 'I hope not – I only came in for a check up.'

113. Worried woman: 'Doctor, I think I'm pregnant.'
Doctor: 'But I gave you the Pill.'
Worried woman: 'Yes, I know. But it keeps falling out.'

114. 'Doctor, doctor! I've just swallowed a spoon.'
'Sit down and don't stir.'

115. 'Doctor, doctor! I'm terribly worried. I keep seeing pink striped crocodiles every time I try to get to sleep.'
'Have you seen a psychiatrist?'
'No – only pink striped crocodiles.'

116. Worried patient: 'Doctor, I'm very worried. I'm still suffering from exhaustion and fatigue when I come home from work every evening.'
Doctor: 'Oh, that's nothing to worry about. Just have a few drinks before your dinner – that will soon wake you up.'
Patient: 'Thanks very much, doctor! But when I consulted you before, you told me to cut out drinking alcohol completely.'
Doctor: 'Yes, so I did. But that was last week, old chap – and medical science has progressed enormously since then.'

117. Grandma was nearly ninety years of age when she won £1,000,000 on the football pools. Her family were extremely worried about her heart and feared that news of her large win would come as too much of a shock for her.
'I think we had better call in the doctor to tell her the news,' suggested the eldest son.
The doctor soon arrived and the situation was explained to him.
'Now, you don't have to worry about anything,' said the doctor. 'I am fully trained in such delicate matters and I feel

sure I can break this news to her gently. I assure you, there is absolutely no need for you to fear for her health. Everything will be quite safe if left to me.'

The doctor went in to see the old lady and gradually brought the conversation around to football pools.

'Tell me,' said the doctor, 'what would you do if you had a large win on the pools – say one million pounds?'

'Why,' replied the old lady, 'I'd give half of it to you, of course.'

The doctor fell down dead with shock.

118. The doctor had just finished examining the very attractive young girl.

Doctor: 'Have you been going out with men, Miss Jones?'

Miss Jones: 'Oh, no, doctor, never!'

Doctor: 'Are you quite sure? Bearing in mind that I've now examined the sample you sent, do you still say you've never had anything to do with men?'

Miss Jones: 'Quite sure, doctor. Can I go now?'

Doctor: 'No.'

Miss Jones: 'But why not?'

Doctor: 'Because, Miss Jones, I'm awaiting the arrival of the Three Wise Men.'

119. Patient: 'And if I take these little green pills exactly as you suggested, will I get better?'

Doctor: 'Well, let's put it this way – none of my patients has ever come back for more of those pills.'

120. Patient: 'I've got a terrible pain in my right arm, doctor.'

Doctor: 'Don't worry, it's just old age.'

Patient: 'But in that case, why doesn't my left arm hurt, too – I've had it just as long?'

121. The senior civil servant went to the doctor and complained of being unable to sleep.

Doctor: 'Oh! Don't you sleep at night?'

Civil servant: 'Yes, I sleep very well at night. And I sleep quite soundly most of the mornings, too – but I find it's very difficult to sleep in the afternoons as well.'

122. Patient: 'And when my right arm is quite better, will I be able to play the trumpet?'

Doctor: 'Most certainly – you should be able to play it with ease.'

Patient: 'That's wonderful – I could never play it before.'

DOGS

123. 'My dog plays chess with me.'

'That's amazing! It must be a really intelligent animal.'

'Not really. I've won three games to two so far this evening.'

124. 'I've just lost my dog.'

'Why don't you put an advertisement in the paper?'

'Don't be silly – my dog can't read.'

125. It was one of the strangest looking dogs they had ever seen at the pub, and the regulars found it a great topic of conversation.

Eventually, one of them sidled over to the dog's owner and said: 'That's a stupid looking dog you've got there. Can it fight?'

'Sure,' replied the owner.

'Well,' said the man. 'I bet you five pounds that my labrador can beat your dog.'

The owner accepted the bet and the labrador was led in to fight. After twenty-two seconds the labrador lay dead on the floor. The loser, looking down at his dead dog, shook his head sadly and said: 'Your dog can certainly fight. But I still think it's a funny looking dog.'

'Yes,' agreed the owner. 'And it looked even funnier until I shaved its mane off.'

126. Man: 'My dog has got no tail.'
  Friend: 'How do you know when it's happy?'
  Man: 'When it stops biting me.'

127. 'That's a lovely bulldog you've got there.'
  'No, it's not a bulldog – it was chasing a cat and ran into a wall.'

128. 'My dog has got no nose.'
  'How does it smell?' -
  'Terrible.'

129. Man: 'I want a dog licence please.'
  Post Office clerk: 'What name?'
  Man: 'Bonzo.'

130. Man: 'Where's your dog?'
  Friend: 'I've had it put down.'
  Man: 'Was it mad?'
  Friend: 'Well, it wasn't exactly pleased.'

131. Man: 'I took my dog to the vet today because it bit my wife.'
  Friend: 'Did you have it put to sleep?'
  Man: 'No, of course not – I had its teeth sharpened.'

DOLPHINS
132. Dolphins are so intelligent that within only a few weeks of being in captivity they can train a man to stand on the very edge of their pool and throw them fish three times a day.

DREAMS
133. Simon was becoming worried about his ever-increasing weight. One day in his club he happened to mention this to his friend, Peter.
  'I can recommend a very good doctor,' said Peter. 'I owe my slimness all to Dr. Frank Einstein. He's invented these marvellous pills which I take.'

40

'It sounds quite amazing,' said Simon. 'But how do they work?'

'It's really psychological. Every night I take two of the pills just before going to sleep and I always dream about being on a South Sea island, surrounded by hordes of beautiful young native girls. And every day I chase them all around the island and when I wake up I seem to have sweated off a few ounces of surplus fat. It's incredible – and enjoyable!'

The following day Simon went to see Dr. Einstein and begged him to give him the same tablets as he was giving Peter. The doctor agreed, and within a few weeks Simon was much thinner.

'How are you finding the treatment?' asked Dr. Einstein, when Simon called in for his regular check-up.

'It's very good. But I do have one complaint.'

'Oh, and what is that?'

'The pills you gave my friend Peter made him have wonderful dreams about chasing young native girls all over an island. But all I seem to get is the same horrible nightmare – being chased all over the island by hungry cannibals. Why can't I have pleasant dreams like Peter?'

'Because,' replied the doctor, 'Peter is a private patient – and you are National Health.'

DRUNKS

134. The landlord of a pub frequented by an extremely heavy drinker opened up one day, and in walked a pink elephant, a green rhinoceros and several orange striped crocodiles. 'I'm sorry,' said the publican, 'I'm afraid he isn't in yet.'

135. The fire engine careered around the corner, and sped off up a road, bells clanging, just as a drunk was staggering out of a pub. He promptly chased after the fire engine, but soon collapsed, exhausted, after only a few hundred yards.

'All right,' he sobbed. 'You can keep your rotten ice lollies!'

136. A drunk came across a man doing press ups in the park, so he said: 'Excuse me, I think someone has stolen your girlfriend.'

137. The drunk came tottering out of a pub and found a man selling tortoises.

'How much are they?' asked the drunk.

'Only five pounds each,' replied the man.

'I'll take one,' said the drunk, and after he had paid for the tortoise he took it and staggered off.

After twenty minutes, the drunk came swaying up to the tortoise seller and bought another tortoise before teetering away again.

Fifteen minutes later the drunk returned to the tortoise seller. 'You know,' he said, as he bought yet another tortoise, 'they're very expensive – but, by jove, I really love your crunchy pies!'

E

ELEPHANT
138. Why are elephants grey? To distinguish them from blackberries.

EMPLOYERS
139. Angry employer: 'Why are you late again this morning?'

Young typist: 'I overslept.'

Angry employer: 'You mean, you sleep at home *as well*?'

140. At the Company Board meeting the Chairman rose to make his speech. 'Who has been carrying on with my secretary?' he demanded.

This was met with silence. 'All right, then,' said the Chairman, 'put it this way – who has *not* been carrying on with my secretary?'

Again there was silence, and then one man said, self-consciously: 'Me, sir.'

'Right,' said the Chairman. '*You* sack her.'

141. Angry employer: 'You should have been here at nine o'clock.'

Late employee: 'Why, what happened?'

ESKIMO
142. What do you call an Eskimo wearing five balaclavas? Anything you like, because he can't hear you.

143. The Eskimo set off in his kayak when he met his Cockney Eskimo friend. The Eskimo said he was very cold and so he made a fire in the bottom of his kayak, but the kayak soon burst into flames and the Eskimo had to be rescued by his friend.

'Why did my kayak go up in flames like that?' asked the Eskimo.

'Simple!' replied his friend. 'You can't hope to have your kayak and 'eat it.'

ESTATE AGENT
144. Estate agent to young house-hunting couple: 'First you tell me what you can afford. Then we'll have a good laugh about it and go on from there.'

EXECUTIVES
145. The managing director's son had just died and as the managing director was without any other heirs there was a mad scramble amongst the executives of the company to take the son's place – even though the son had not yet been laid to rest.

One of the executives was so ambitious that he called on the managing director to express his sympathy at the sad loss of such a great man. But he continued: 'No one could ever hope to achieve as much as your son has done – but I wondered, sir, if it would be possible for me to take his place.'

'Certainly,' replied the managing director. 'I'll see if the undertaker can arrange it.'

146. The television company decided to make a programme about successful business executives, so they called five of them into the studio to talk about their lives and how they managed to be so successful.

The first four executives all told of how they had fought to get to the top – all four of them marrying their respective boss's daughter. But the fifth executive had had a really hard fight to become successful. 'Life was never very easy for me,' he explained. 'I had to fight for everything and times were often extremely difficult – but I just gritted my teeth, rolled up my sleeves . . . and got down to asking Dad to lend me another £50,000.'

EYELASHES

147. False eyelashes are a marvellous invention – I spent half an hour in the bathroom trying to kill one of the damn things.

F

FEATHERS

148. Young girl: 'If you kiss me it will be a feather in my cap.'

Handsome young man: 'Come outside and I'll make you a Red Indian Chief.'

FLEAS

149. The male flea said to the pretty female flea: 'Come up and see my itchings.'

150. The two fleas were just leaving the theatre when the male flea turned to the female flea and said: 'Shall we walk, or take a dog?'

151. The old flea was travelling to the cinema on his snail when he was overtaken by a young flea tearing along on a slug.

'What has happened to your old snail?' asked the old flea.

'Oh,' shouted the young flea, gradually disappearing into the distance, 'I thought I'd part exchange it for a convertible.'

FLIES

152. How do you keep flies out of the kitchen? Put a bucket of manure in the lounge.

FLYING

153. The aeroplane was so old it even had an outside lavatory.

154. The bearded man stuck a gun in the pilot's back and hissed: 'Take me to London.'

Pilot: 'But we're supposed to be going to London, anyway.'

Bearded man: 'I know. But I've been hi-jacked to Cuba twice before, so this time I'm taking no chances.'

FOOD

155. 'Waiter, can I have some undercooked chips, some gooey, cold beans and a fried egg coated in old grease?'

'I'm sorry sir, but we couldn't possibly give you anything like that.'

'Why not? That's what you gave me yesterday.'

156. 'Waiter! What are these coins doing in my soup?'

'Well, sir, you said you would stop coming to this restaurant unless there was change in the meals.'

157. Waiter: 'And how did you find the meat, sir?'
Customer: 'Oh, I just lifted up a chip and there it was.'

158. 'And how do you like the meat balls?'
'I don't know – I've never been to any.'

159. Candles make light meals.

160. Customer: 'There's only one piece of meat on my plate.'
Waiter: 'Wait a minute, sir, and I'll cut it in two.'

161. 'Waiter! This coffee tastes like mud.'
'Well, sir, it was ground only ten minutes ago.'

162. A man was visiting London when he saw an advertisement for a restaurant which claimed that any dish requested could be served.

The man decided to visit this restaurant in order to test the validity of their claims. When he was seated at his table he asked the waiter for elephant ears on toast. The waiter took this order calmly, and went away into the kitchens.

A few minutes later the waiter returned and said: 'I do apologize, sir, but we've run out of bread.'

163. 'I don't think much of your wife.'
'Never mind – eat the vegetables instead.'

164. I eat small pieces of metal every day. It's my staple diet.

165. I rose early this morning – I ate some yeast last night.

166. Eat Arthur's Arsenic – and you'll never live to regret it.

167. 'Waiter! There's a button in my salad.'
'Oh! It must have come off the salad dressing.'

168. 'Waiter! Is this food pure?'
'As pure as the girl of your dreams, sir.'
'Oh! Then I'd rather not have it, thanks.'

169. A man was amazed to find a restaurant advertising: 'Chicken dinners – only 10p.'

He decided to try one of these dinners so he paid his 10p and his taste buds began to anticipate the pleasant chicken dinner that was to come – until the waiter brought him a plate of corn.

170. He had jelly in one ear and custard in the other, so he told everyone to speak up as he was a trifle deaf.

171. 'Waiter! This egg is bad.'
'Don't blame me. I only lay the table.'

172. 'Waiter! This plate is damp.'
'Yes, I know, sir. That's the soup.'

173. 'Waiter! There's a dead spider in my soup.'
'Yes, I know, sir. It's the heat that kills them.'

174. When I lived in lodgings my landlady kept some animals in the yard at the back of the house.

The first day I was there, one of the chickens died, so we had chicken soup.

The next day, the pig died, so I was offered pork chops.

The following day, the duck died, so we had roast duck with apple sauce.

The next day my landlady's husband died – so I left.

G

GAMBLING

175. The compulsive gambler at the roulette table was having a particularly bad run of luck when suddenly he heard a soft, ghostly voice in his ear say 'Number Seven'.

The gambler furtively looked behind him, but there was no one near him who could possibly have made such a ghostly whisper. The gambler decided he had nothing to lose by backing the advice of the mysterious whisperer.

The number came up – number seven had won the gambler a small sum of money – but not enough to cover his earlier losses, so the gambler continued at the table. Again, the ghostly voice whispered 'Number Seven', and the gambler followed the advice and won yet again.

This went on for some considerable time. Just before the gambler placed each bet the ghostly voice would whisper: 'Number Seven', and the number seven always came up.

After this had happened nine times in succession, the gambler had collected quite a number of interested spectators – as well as winning well over five thousand pounds.

Then the ghostly voice whispered: 'Put everything on Number Five.' The gambler was surprised at the change in directions, but he decided to continue to follow the advice given him by the strange, ghostly voice.

The roulette wheel spun round, the gambler held his breath, the crowd around the table watched with astonishment – and the ball landed in number seven. And the ghostly voice in the gambler's ear said 'Damn!'

GERMS

176. 'Did you know that deep breathing kills germs?'
'Yes. But how do you get them to breathe deeply?'

GOLDFISH

177. The philosophical goldfish swam around in his bowl, then stopped for a few seconds and turned to his companion and asked: 'Do you believe in the existence of God?'

'Yes,' replied the second goldfish. 'Who else do you suppose changes our water?'

GRAVE DIGGER

178. The eminent surgeon was walking through his local churchyard one day when he saw the grave digger having a rest and drinking from a bottle of beer.

'Hey, you!' called the surgeon. 'How dare you laze about and drink alcohol in the churchard! Get on with your job, or I shall complain to the vicar.'

'I should have thought you'd be the last person to complain,' said the grave digger, 'bearing in mind all your blunders I've had to cover up.'

H

HAMSTER

179. The man was lonely so he went to his local petshop and asked for an animal that would make a good companion for him as he was allergic to birds and fish. The petshop owner recommended a hamster, so the man bought two hamsters, some hamster food, and a special cage.

The next day the man was back in the petshop. 'Those two hamsters you sold me have died. There must have been something wrong with them. Can I have two more, please?'

The petshop owner gave him two more hamsters and the man left the shop. But next day the man returned and said: 'This is ridiculous! The two hamsters you gave me yesterday fell down and died this morning. I'll buy your entire stock of hamsters — then perhaps I might get two that will live a reasonable length of time — and perhaps even breed and keep me amused.'

The petshop owner sold the man his complete stock of hamsters — all fifty-eight of them — and the man left the petshop.

Two days later the petshop owner was horrified to find the man in his shop again. 'All the hamsters have died,' said the man. 'I don't want anything to do with animals ever again — they just seem to curl up and die just to spite me. But it seems a pity to waste all the hamster bodies — is there anything you can suggest to do with them? It seems horrible to have to throw them in the dustbin.'

'Well,' said the petshop owner, 'if you mash them all up and then boil them until you get a sort of gooey stuff, this makes excellent fertilizer for the garden.'

The man left the shop and went home to follow the petshop owner's instructions. But a week later the man was back in the petshop. 'I really must congratulate you on your excellent suggestion,' said the man. 'I did as you suggested with the hamster bodies and in no time at all I had seven gigantic beanstalks in my garden. In fact, they were so high I had to stick red lights on top of them to warn aeroplanes to keep away. That hamster mixture really is amazing stuff for beanstalks.'

'You know,' said the petshop owner. 'That's incredible. You usually get Tulips From Hamster Jam.'

HEDGEHOG
180. Hedgehog finding itself on top of a scrubbing brush: 'We all make mistakes, don't we?'

HEREAFTER
181. The small car pulled up to a sudden halt. 'Have you run out of petrol?' asked the girl, somewhat sarcastically.

'No, of course not,' replied her young male companion.

'Then why have we stopped?'

'You will no doubt have noticed that we are parked in a secluded spot in the middle of this forest and miles from anywhere – so I thought you might like a discussion about the hereafter.'

'That's something new,' replied the young girl. 'What do you mean?'

'Simple! If you're not hereafter what I'm hereafter, you'll be hereafter I've gone.'

HISTORICAL
182. 'Apart from *that*, Mrs. Lincoln, how did you enjoy the play?'

183. At the time of the French Revolution many people went completely off their heads.

184. 'Here are the chains I want posted today.'
    'Chains?'
    'Yes. Haven't you heard of chain mail?'

185. One day, during one of the ancient wars, a lusty Roman soldier broke into a house where he found two beautiful maidens and their matronly servant.

'Prepare thyself for a conquest, my dears,' roared the soldier.

The girls fell to their knees and pleaded with him: 'Do with us as thou desire, sir, but please spare our faithful old servant.'

'Shut thy mouth,' snapped the servant. 'War is war.'

186. 'Now, how much would *you* like to contribute to the Indian Relief Fund, Mrs. Custer?'

187. With the African having been captured, Caesar decided to put him in the Arena to fight.

First he was matched against a hungry lion, but the Negro calmly picked up the animal as it rushed towards him, whirled it around in the air by its tail, and then smashed its head in.

The promoters of the fight were annoyed, so the Negro was given a choice. Either fight a pack of lions or enter into combat with their best gladiator.

But the promoters knew the audience wanted to see blood – the blood of the Negro, so as a slight handicap the man was buried up to his neck in sand. The gladiator approached, drew his six foot long sword, raised it above the Negro's head – to an enormous cheer from the audience – then brought it down, but the Negro moved his head to one side so the sword hit the ground.

The crowd rose to their feet, jeering and shouting: 'Fight fair, you coward!'

188. Then there was the ancient fireplace salesman – Alfred the *Grate*!

189. Paul Revere came thundering up to a small farmhouse during his historic ride from Boston to Lexington. The young farmer's wife came to the door.

'Get ya husband,' yelled Revere, 'we gotta fight the English.'

'My husband ain't home,' she replied, trembling.

'Get ya sons and kinfolk,' he yelled.

'I ain't got no sons nor kinfolk.'

'Ain't nobody at home?'

'Nope!'

'Whoah, boy!'

HOLIDAYS

190. Two little boys were paddling in the sea at Margate.

'Coo, ain't your feet dirty,' said one little boy.

'Yes,' replied the other, 'we didn't come last year.'

HOLLYWOOD

191. Two little boys were talking in Hollywood. 'What's your new dad like?' asked one.

'Oh, he's O.K., I guess,' replied the other. 'Have you met him?'

'Yeah!' said the first boy. 'We had him last year.'

192. The Hollywood props department manager answered his 'phone only to hear the producer bawl at him: 'Why haven't you got me the full-scale mock up of the inside of the Titanic like I asked for yesterday? And where are the fifty-six stuffed penguins I asked for this morning? How the hell do you expect me to make a film about King Canute without the props I ask for?'

'But . . . but . . .' stammered the props manager.

'Don't "but . . . but . . ." me!' roared the producer. 'Nobody on this film seems to care about accuracy and realism except me. Now, get me those props or . . .'

'But if you keep shouting all the time,' soothed the props manager, 'you'll get ulcers and . . .'

'I don't *get* ulcers!' roared the producer. 'I *give* them!'

54

HOSPITAL

193. Nurse: 'Well, Mr. Mitchell, you seem to be coughing much more easily this morning.'

Mr. Mitchell, groaning in his bed: 'That's because I've been practising all night.'

194. 1st patient: 'I see they've brought in another case of diarrhoea.'

2nd patient: 'That's good! Anything is better than that awful lemonade they've been giving us.'

HOTELS

195. Tom was explaining to his friends how bad the hotel situation was in America. 'Once the manager showed me to my room and said: "Here you are, sir, complete with running water." I left immediately, insulted. After all, why should he think I wanted to sleep with a Red Indian?'

196. Notice in a foreign hotel: 'The water in this establishment is completely hygienic – it has all been passed by the manager.'

197. It was one o'clock in the morning and the manager of the hotel had just been woken up by a frantic 'phone call from a little old lady. 'Come quickly! Oh, please come quickly!' she wailed. 'I can see a naked man from my window.'

The manager hastily dressed and rushed up to the little old lady's room. He found her pointing at a block of flats opposite her hotel bedroom – but all the manager could see was the naked top half of a young man.

'But my dear woman,' soothed the manager, 'the young man opposite is surely only preparing for bed. And how can you possibly be offended by him? The man may not be completely naked.'

'The wardrobe!' shrieked the little old lady. 'Stand on the wardrobe.'

198. The beautiful young girl was lying naked on the roof of her expensive hotel, sunbathing. Suddenly the manager came up to her, coughed slightly, then said: 'Excuse me, madam, but this is hardly the place for nudity.'

'Why not?' asked the girl. 'I can't see anyone.'

'That may be so,' replied the manager, 'but you are lying on the skylight over the dining room and it is now lunch time.'

HYPOCHONDRIAC
199. Inscription on the tombstone of a hypochondriac: 'See – I *told* you I was ill.'

I

IMPRESSIONS

200. Jim's wife was chatting to her friend about Jim's boss, who at that moment was regaling the party with details of his war experiences in Egypt.

'I believe he's great at doing impressions,' commented the friend.

'Yes,' agreed Jim's wife. 'Right now he's doing his impression of a river – small at the head and big at the mouth.'

INSECTS

201. It was the greatest football game of the century – the mice against the insects.

The insect team marched on to the field with only ten men. Shortly after, the mice scuttled on to the pitch and the game began. Within minutes, the insects were beaten back into a defensive position.

By the time the whistle for the first half was blown the insects were losing by eighteen goals to nil.

When the second half began the elventh member of the insect team marched on to the field. He soon began to score goal after goal for the insect team and by the end of the game the insects had won by nineteen goals to eighteen.

'That was a great game,' said the captain of the mice, 'but you could have really slaughtered us if you had brought on your eleventh man at the start of the game. Why didn't you?'

'Oh,' replied the insect captain, turning to the eleventh player, a centipede, 'we couldn't bring him on at the start as he was still putting on his boots. It does take him a long time, you know!'

202. Little Wilhelmina was in the garden when she asked: 'Dad – what are those two insects doing?'

'Well,' said her father, 'you know what I told you about the birds and bees – that's what they are doing.'

'But they are not birds and bees.'

'I know – they're called daddy-longlegs.'

'Oh!' said Wilhelmina, and paused to think about this for a while. Then she said: 'So one is a mummy-longlegs and the other a daddy-longlegs.'

'No,' replied her father. 'They're both daddy-longlegs.'

Wilhelmina thought for a while, then stamped on the insects.

'What did you do that for?' asked her father, somewhat surprised.

'I'm not having *that* sort of thing in *our* garden,' said Wilhelmina, firmly.

IRISH

203. Man: 'My sister married an Irishman.'
    Friend: 'Oh, really?'
    Man: 'No, O'Reilly.'

204. The Irishman died and went to Heaven. He knocked at the Pearly Gates, but no one answered. He knocked again and shouted: 'Hey, let me in! I'm Paddy Murphy and I've been sent to Heaven.'

Eventually St. Peter appeared and looked through the Gates at the Irishman and said: 'Go away – I'm not going to make stew just for one.'

205. He was a sort of Irish/Jewish gnome – so they called him a lepra-Cohen.

206. Jesus was to have been born in Ireland – until God had difficulty finding even one wise man, let alone three.

207. Three Irishmen were walking along a road when a young man in a battered sports car ran over them. He got out of his car and buried them in a field. Then he went to a police station to report what he had done.

'I'm terribly sorry, officer,' he said, 'but I've just run over three Irishmen and so I buried them in a field.'

'Are you sure they were dead?' asked the policeman.

'Well,' said the young man, 'two said they weren't – but you know what liars Irishmen are.'

208. An Irishman was stopped at the Customs after returning from a holiday on the Continent.

'What's this in this bottle?' asked the customs officer, taking out a large bottle from the Irishman's suitcase.

'Oh,' said the Irishman, 'that is only Holy Water from Lourdes.'

'Hmmm!' muttered the customs officer as he took the top off the bottle and sniffed the liquid inside. Then he tasted some of it. 'It looks, smells and tastes very much like whisky to me, sir.'

'Glory be!' replied the Irishman, ' 'tis another miracle!'

209. It was pouring with rain and the old man fell down, dying, in the gutter. A man saw this and rushed up to help.

'What can I do? Where do you live? What's your name?' asked the man.

'Seamus O'Reilly,' replied the old man. 'I'm dying. There's nothing you can do to help.'

'But shall I fetch the priest?'

'No, fetch the rabbi.'

'Did I hear you right?' asked the man. 'With a name like Seamus O'Reilly and an accent like yours, you want me to fetch the rabbi and not the priest?'

'Yes,' replied the old man. 'I wouldn't bring the priest out on a night like this.'

210. It was the annual meeting of the international brotherhood of space scientists in 1997.

'We are preparing to send a rocket to Pluto,' announced the Americans, proudly. 'It will have six men aboard and will stay on Pluto for a whole month before making the long trip back to Earth.'

'That's nothing!' scoffed the Russians. 'We are almost ready to launch our spaceship containing two hundred men and women to start the first colony on Uranus.'

'Our country can beat you both,' said the Irish scientist. 'We are going to send a rocket straight to the Sun.'

'Don't be silly,' said the American and Russian scientists, 'the rocket will melt before it gets there.'

'No it won't,' replied the Irish scientist. 'We're sending it up at night.'

ITALIAN ARMY

211. It was quite a number of years ago when the Italian Army used to fight with spears. Just before one of their greatest battles, the Italian commander assembled his men to give them a stirring speech before they went into battle.

'It does not matter,' he said, 'that the odds are overwhelmingly against us. We are Italians and we shall go forward fighting as only Italians can. Now raise up your spears and come with me into battle. I will lead the way to a glorious victory that shall be ours.'

As the commander picked up his spear and marched bravely forwards to meet the enemy, his men laid down their spears, sat on the ground, clapped their hands, and shouted: 'Bravo!'

J

JAPANESE

212. An ancient Japanese General and an old British Major were talking.

'Why do you always win battles, whereas we always seem to lose all our wars, except the economic ones?' asked the Japanese General.

'Because we always pray to God before we go into battle,' replied the British Major.

'That's not so, because we also pray to God – but we never win.'

'Ah!' said the British Major, 'but not everyone can understand Japanese.'

JEWISH

213. 'I think the War between Israel and Egypt is about to start all over again.'

'What makes you think that?'

'Because the Egyptians are having all their tanks rebuilt with reversing lights.'

214. Levi went to the Jewish burial ground and asked the rabbi if he could bury a cat. The rabbi was horrified. 'You, a good Jew, want to bury a cat in the graveyard,' he said. 'Certainly not!'

'Then I can't give you the ten thousand pounds it left the synagogue in its will,' replied Levi, sadly.

'Oh!' said the rabbi. 'Why didn't you say it was a Jewish cat?'

215. The Jewish football match was decided at the toss of a Cohen.

216. The newly opened shopping centre had three tailors – all with shops next to each other. As another coincidence, all three tailors were named Jacob Silverstein.

The first tailor put up a sign over his shop which proclaimed: 'Jacob Silverstein – High Class Tailor.'

The second tailor put up a sign saying: 'Silverstein – the tailor of distinction.'

The third tailor put up a smaller notice above his shop, but it said: 'Silverstein's Tailors – Main Entrance.'

217. Rachel and Rebecca met in the small cafe to talk over old times, as they had not seen each other for several years.

'And how are your three sons?' asked Rebecca.

'Well,' replied Rachel, 'the first, he is in property and owns large pieces of London. The second, he is a world famous brain surgeon. And the third, he is the really intellectual one.'

'But what does he do?' asked Rebecca. 'What does he earn?'

'He studies an awful lot and he is a rabbi. He earns about a thousand pounds a year.'

'Only a thousand a year as a rabbi?' said Rebecca, astonished. 'What kind of a job is that for a Jewish boy?'

218. Jacob was dying and the family gathered around his bedside.

'Mama,' he whispered.

'I'm here, Jacob,' she replied.

'Rachel,' he sighed.

'I'm here, Papa.'

'Isaac!'

'I'm here, Papa.'

'Levi?' he coughed.

'I'm here, too, Papa.'

'Then,' he wheezed, 'who the hell is minding the shop?'

219. The German officer in command of the prison camp thought that, as it was Christmas Eve, he would set some of his prisoners free. He decided that the fairest way would be to

ask each prisoner a question, and those who answered correctly would be allowed to escape.

The first prisoner to be interviewed was a British officer and the German officer asked: 'In 1912 a famous ship collided vith an iceberg. Vot vos its name?'

'The Titanic,' replied the British officer, and he was promptly released.

The next prisoner was an American. The German officer asked: 'In 1912 der Titanic sank van it vos in collision vith an iceberg. How many lives ver lost?'

'1,517,' replied the American, and he was set free.

The third prisoner to appear was Jewish. 'In 1912,' said the German, 'der Titanic collided vith an iceberg and sank vith der loss of 1,517 lives. Vot ver their names?'

220. Is the Chief Rabbi of the Eskimos called Eskimoses?

221. Abe rushed round to Samuel's house, extremely distressed. 'De most terrible thing just happened. I meet my son off de plane this morning and he says to me, "Papa," he says, "I've been converted. I'm a Christian." '

Samuel listened in silence, then said, quietly, 'Vell, de same thing happened to me. I, too, just met my son off de ship and he too has been converted. Vot shall ve do?'

They decided to consult the rabbi but, alas, his son had suddenly been converted. So, in desperation, the three men went to the synagogue and prayed as they had never prayed before.

After a while there was a great crash of thunder and a voice boomed: 'Gentlemen, you know vot? I had de same trouble myself.'

222. Abe walked into a restaurant and ordered a meal.

'I'm afraid we can't serve you, sir,' said the waiter.

'Vy not?' asked Abe.

'On the manager's instructions, sir.'

'Then let me speak to the manager.'

The manager duly comes to Abe's table and announces: 'I'm the manager, Harry Cohen.'

'Look,' said Abe, 'you're obviously Jewish yet you refuse to serve Jews. Why?'

'Have you ever tasted our food?' asked the manager.

223. 'Why do Jews always answer a question with a question?'

'Vell, vy not?'

224. Definition of circumcision: that which cuts off the Jews from the Gentiles.

225. It was during the Arab/Israeli troubles. The Egyptians were having some trouble with a sniper, so they sent out a party of ten men to deal with him.

A few days passed, and there was no sign of the ten men who had been sent out, and yet the sniper was still firing away. The Egyptians decided to send out a whole platoon to deal with the sniper.

The Egyptians all went marching out – but a few hours later only one of them came staggering back. 'The rest are all dead,' he reported. 'But it's a trick – a typical Jewish trick – there's two of them.'

JOURNALIST

226. 'Robert!' shouted the editor of the local newspaper. 'Did you get that story about the man who sings bass and soprano at the same time?'

'There's no story, sir,' replied Robert, the young reporter. 'The man has two heads.'

JUDGES

227. Most judges wear a little wig on each ear. This is known as an ear wig.

228. The judge found the blacksmith guilty of forging.

229. The judge was only four feet three inches tall – a small thing sent to try us.

230. The judge gave the man who stole a calendar twelve months.

K

KANGAROO

231. One enterprising Australian farmer tried to cross a kangaroo with a sheep so he would get a woolly jumper.

232. The mother kangaroo suddenly leapt into the air and gave a cry of pain and anguish. 'Sidney!' she screamed. 'How many more times do I have to tell you that you cannot smoke in bed!'

KNOCK KNOCK

233. 'Knock, knock.'
  'Who's there?'
  'Adolf.'
  'Adolf who?'
  'A dolf ball hid me in der moud and dat's why I talk fuddy.

234. 'Knock, knock.'
  'Who's there?'
  'The invisible man.'
  'Well, tell him I can't see him.'

235. 'Knock, knock.'
  'Who's there?'
  'Irish stew.'
  'Irish stew who?'
  'Irish stew in the name of the law.'

236. 'Knock, knock.'
  'Who's there?'
  'You're a lady.'
  'You're a lady who?'
  'I didn't know you could yodel.'

L

LANDLORD

237. The young man walked into the petshop and asked if he could buy 387 beetles, 18 rats and five mice.

'I'm sorry, sir, but we can only supply the mice. But what did you want all the other creatures for?' asked the petshop manager.

'I was thrown out of my flat this morning,' replied the young man. 'And my landlord says I must leave the place exactly as I found it.'

LEBANON

238. Why didn't the Lebanon bomb Israel during the Seven-Day War? Because the pilot was ill.

LEGAL

239. The scene is a law court. The prosecution counsel faces the female witness and rasps: 'Is it true you committed adultery on the 18th of June in a snowstorm while riding on the roof of an automobile travelling at ninety miles an hour through Slough with a one-legged dwarf waving a Union Jack?'

The young woman in the witness box looked straight at the prosecuting counsel and said, calmly: 'What was the date again?'

240. Judge: 'Did you sleep with this woman?'
Man in witness box: 'No, your honour, not a wink.'

241. Policeman in witness box: This woman came up to me when I was in plain clothes and tried to pass off this five pound note, m'lud.'
Judge: 'Counterfeit?'
Policeman in witness box: 'Yes, m'lud, she had two.'

242. The judge had just finished telling the prisoner that he

was free to go as the jury had found him not guilty of fraud, so the prisoner asked: 'Does that mean I can keep the money?'

LIARS
243. Man: 'That damn wife of mine is a liar!'
Friend: 'How do you know?'
Man: 'Because she said she spent the night with Claire.'
Friend: 'So?'
Man: '*I* spent the night with Claire.'

244. 'I can't stop telling lies.'
'I don't believe you.'

245. Women are to blame for all the lying men do – they will insist on continually asking questions.

LION
246. One day the lion woke up feeling better than he had ever done before. He felt so fit and healthy he could beat the world. So he rose proudly and went for a prowl in the jungle. Soon he came across a snake and the lion stopped.

'Who is the king of the jungle?' asked the lion.

'You, of course,' replied the snake, and slithered away.

Next, the lion came to a small pool where he found a crocodile.

'Who is the king of the jungle?'

'Why, you are,' replied the crocodile and slid into the murky depths of the water.

This went on all morning, all the animals agreeing that the lion was king of the jungle. Then he came across an elephant.

'Who is the king of the jungle?' asked the lion.

In reply, the elephant picked up the lion with its trunk, hurled the lion around in the air and then bashed him against the ground and stamped on him.

'All right, all right,' groaned the battered lion. 'There's no need to get angry just because you don't know the answer.'

247. Then there was the man-eating lion who was killed in one of the ancient Roman games. It had forgotten to wear its after-slave potion.

LUMBERJACK

248. James was a very old man and when he turned up at a Canadian lumberjacks' camp and asked if he could help in chopping down the trees no one would take him seriously.

'Let me show you how good I am,' begged the old man.

Eventually, the lumberjack boss got tired of the old man's whining and pleading and gave James an axe, saying: 'Don't try too hard, old man. We don't want you killing yourself.'

James took the axe and went over to one of the tallest trees near the camp. The lumberjacks were amazed to see the old man chop away at the tree with enormous speed, and within only a few minutes the tree was lying on the ground.

'That's amazing!' said the lumberjack boss. 'Where did you learn to chop trees down like that?'

'I got my basic training in the Sahara,' replied the old man.

'But there aren't any trees in the Sahara,' said the lumberjack boss.

'That's right,' replied the old man. 'But there used to be until I started training.'

M

MAGICIAN

249. A magician on board a cruise ship used to do amazing tricks every night in the cabaret spot – but the captain's pet parrot always used to shout 'Phoney, phoney!' at the end of the magician's act.

Then one day the ship hit an iceberg and sank, but the magician and the parrot managed to cling to a piece of wood and float clear of the sinking ship.

After a few days of floating, the parrot turned an inquisitive beak to the magician and said: 'O.K., genius. What have you done with the ship?'

MARRIED LIFE

250. Married man: 'In your sermon this morning, vicar, you said it was wrong for people to profit from other people's mistakes. Do you really agree with that?'

Vicar: 'Of course I do.'

Married man: 'In that case, will you consider refunding the ten pounds I paid you for marrying me to my wife seven years ago?'

251. My wife has had her face lifted so many times that now they have to lower her body.

252. My wife and I never argue. She always goes her way and I always go hers.

253. My wife is so cross eyed that every time she cries the tears run down her back. The doctor said it was Back Teria.

254. My wife is so jealous and suspicious that even her eyes watch each other.

255. My wife is so frigid whenever she opens her mouth a little light comes on.

256. David was out all night with the glamorous hostess from a notorious Soho night club. When he returned home at five o'clock in the morning he tried to sneak into bed with his wife without waking her. But he was unsuccessful and she turned on the bedside light and watched her husband undress before putting on his pyjamas.

'Where is your underwear?' she demanded, when it was obvious that David had not been wearing any even before he had started to undress.

'My God!' cried David, in anguish. 'I've been robbed!'

257. Wife: Darling what would you do if you came home from the office one day and found me in bed with another man?'

Husband: 'Oh, I'd tell him to go away and beat him over the head with his white stick.'

258. I wouldn't say my wife had tired blood – but she tried to commit suicide twice by cutting her throat – but nothing happened.

259. I wouldn't say my wife is continually moaning about being ill, but she's just bought a Do-It-Yourself Embalming Kit.

260. I wouldn't say my wife was promiscuous, but she's been picked up so many times she's beginning to grow handles.

261. That middle-aged couple just across the road from us haven't spoken to each other for ten years. It's not because they've had a row – but they just can't think of anything to say.

262. Her husband is a fascinating conversationalist – if you happen to be interested in building model railways out of matchsticks.

263. My wife has a slight impediment in her speech. Every now and then she has to stop to take a breath.

264. Man: 'My wife and I had a short row on Friday night. She wanted to go to the opera and I wanted to go to the theatre – but we soon came to an agreement.'

Friend: 'And what was the opera like?'

265. At least my wife isn't two-faced. She can't be – otherwise she wouldn't wear that one all the time.

266. And she's got a marvellous old mother. She's 79 and hasn't got one grey hair. She's completely bald.

267. Newly married wife: 'Darling, the woman next door has got a coat exactly like mine.'

Husband: 'I suppose that's a hint that you want a new coat?'

Wife: 'Well, it would be quite a lot cheaper than moving to a new house.'

268. I wouldn't say my wife pushed much dirt under the carpet – but I have to walk uphill to the fireplace.

269. A woman threatened her husband with divorce if he continued to chase after other women. The husband begged forgiveness and solemnly swore not to pay any attention to women other than his wife.

He managed to keep his promise for a few months, but then his wife discovered him kissing a female midget.

'I'm terribly sorry,' apologized the man to his wife, 'but you must admit that I'm tapering off a bit.'

270. My wife is so bandy she hangs her drawers over a boomerang every night.

271. I wouldn't say my wife is a bad cook – but she's the only woman I know who can make an omelette without breaking the eggs.

272. I wouldn't say my husband was stupid – but when he went to a mindreader they gave him his money back.

273. My husband is so thin whenever he goes to the park the ducks throw *him* bread.

274. My wife says I'm effeminate. Compared to her, I suppose I am.

275. The married couple arrived late one night at a hotel, only to be told by the manager: 'I'm sorry, but we're full up – but you can have the bridal suite.'

'But we've been married for more than fifty years,' said the husband.

'So?' said the manager. 'I can let you have the ballroom – but you don't *have* to dance.'

276. My wife is something of an actress. She spends the summer season swimming up and down Loch Ness.

277. My husband is so stupid he even takes a saddle to bed with him in case he has nightmares.

278. 'Jean, I think your husband dresses nattily.'
'Natalie who?'

279. It wasn't until after I married my wife that I discovered she was really a redhead – no hair, just a red head.

280. My wife frequently goes for a tramp in the woods – fortunately for him, he always manages to get away.

281. My wife, besides being rather fat, is incredibly bossy – always telling people what they should do. One day she was on a bus and had just settled down and got comfortable in her seat when she saw that the only standing passengers were three middle-aged women.

My wife turned to the man sitting next to her and said, in a very loud voice: 'If you were a gentleman, you'd get up and let one of those women sit down.'

'If you were a lady,' said the man, 'you'd get up and let all three of them sit down.'

MARTIAN
282. The two Martians met while on an expedition to Earth.

'Hello,' said the first Martian. 'I'm ZX 6789654.'

'I'm TR 5467892,' said the second Martian.

'That's funny,' said ZX 6789654, 'you don't look Jewish.'

MISSIONARY

283. A missionary went to a remote part of the world to teach some natives. On his travels he came to a small village where he decided to make a speech. It went something like this:

Missionary: 'All men are your enemies and you must love your enemies.'

The natives raised their spears and shouted 'Hussanga!'

Missionary: 'If a man should smite you, turn the other cheek.'

The natives raised their spears again and shouted 'Hussanga!'

Missionary: 'Fighting is wrong – you must not fight.'

Once again, the natives raised their spears and shouted 'Hussanga!'

The missionary decided he had said enough for one day, and as he made his way off the platform he said to the native nearest to him: 'I think my little speech went down quite well, don't you? You all seemed to agree with it.'

'Hmm,' said the native. 'Mind you don't tread in the hussanga when you get off the platform.'

284. It was the old missionary in Africa who gave the tribe of cannibals their first taste of Christianity.

MOUNTAINEERING

285. Two men were climbing a particularly difficult mountain when one of them suddenly fell down a crevasse 500 feet deep.

'Are you all right Bert?' called the man at the top of the crevasse.

'I'm still alive, thank goodness, Fred,' came the reply.

'Here, grab this rope,' said Fred, throwing a rope down to Bert.

'I can't grab it,' shouted Bert. 'My arms are broken.'

'Well, fit it around your legs.'

'I'm afraid I can't do that either,' apologized Bert. 'My legs are broken.'

'Put the rope in your mouth,' shouted Fred.

So Bert put the rope in his mouth and Fred began to haul him to safety. 490 feet ... 400 feet ... 300 feet ... 200 feet ... 100 feet ... 50 feet ... and then Fred called: 'Are you all right, Bert?'

'Yeh-h-h ... h ... h ...'

MOUSE

286. What is the largest species of mouse in the world? A hippapotamouse.

287. What do you get if you cross a mouse with an elephant? Giant holes in the skirting board.

288. A baby mouse saw a bat for the first time in its life and ran home, screaming, to its mother saying it had just seen an angel.

MUMMY,—MUMMY

289. 'Mummy, mummy! The milkman's at the door. Have you got the money – or shall I go out and play?'

290. 'Mummy, mummy! I keep going round in circles.'
'Shut up – or I'll nail your other leg to the floor.'

291. 'Mummy, mummy! I hate daddy's guts.'
'Well, dear, just leave them on the side of your plate.'

292. 'Mummy, mummy! It's getting hot in here – can I come out?'
'No, of course not! Do you want the fire to spread to the rest of the house?'

N

NAILS

293. Man: 'I cured my son of biting his nails.'
Friend: 'Oh, how?'
Man: 'Knocked all his teeth out.'

294. Customer: 'Ironmonger! Have you got one inch nails?'
Ironmonger: 'Yes, sir.'
Customer: 'Then please scratch my back, it's itching something awful.

295. The guest was staring at the child with astonishment as the child busily knocked nails into the expensive Scandinavian furniture in his host's dining-room.

The guest turned to his host and asked: 'Don't you find it expensive to let your son play games like that?'

'Not at all,' replied the host, proudly, 'I get the nails wholesale.'

NELSON

296. Nelson was dying on board H.M.S. *Victory*. He looked up, sadly, and said: 'Kiss me, Hardy!'

Hardy looked down and muttered: 'All these years on the same ship and *now* he asks me!'

NEWS

297. A well-known iron gate manufacturer was said today to be somewhat overwrought.

298. The marriage of the two lighthouse keepers was said this evening to be on the rocks.

299. A Californian scientist has recently invented saw-edged false teeth for eating canned fruit.

300. On Tuesday a man fell into a tank of beer and came to a bitter end.

301. The disappearance of some yeast from a Glasgow bakery in the early hours of this morning has given rise to some anxiety.

302. Missing: Three old ladies – believed to be locked in a lavatory.

303. Owing to a strike at the meteorological office, there will be no weather tomorrow.

304. A man swallowed a dud coin late last night. He is expected to be charged with passing counterfeit money later today.

305. In court this morning was a young man accused of peddling drugs. He said he had left his bicycle at home.

306. A man who beat his carpet to death a few hours ago is soon expected to be charged with matricide.

307. The newly elected mayor laid a foundation stone this afternoon. He is not officially recognized as being a chicken.

308. A man tried to stab me early this evening. He was a man after my own heart.

309. A beautiful young typist kissed a Prince last night. He turned into a toad.

310. In Moscow early this week, Vladimir Baronovitch lifted over two tons – and earned the title: 'The World's Most Perfectly Ruptured Man.'

311. Speaking about the droppings of pigeons in the town, a council official said: 'We must try not to dodge the issue.'

312. The Chairman of a major blotting paper company announced a few minutes ago that he found his work very absorbing.

313. The President of the Periscope Manufacturers' Association said today that business was 'looking up'.

314. Eggs are going up – the hens have lost all sense of direction.

315. A dumpling was said today to be in a bit of a stew.

316. The plan to wrap all meat pies in tin has been foiled.

317. A man walked through the streets of Southampton today wearing only a newspaper. He said he liked to dress with *The Times*.

318. An inflatable rubber lilo collapsed and died today at its South Harrow home.

319. It has recently been discovered that Wales is sinking into the sea – due to the many leeks in the ground.

320. A strawberry was reported today to be in a bit of a jam.

321. It was reported this afternoon that a man in Cornwall was partially electrocuted. After his recovery the man said: 'It came as something of a shock.'

322. Yesterday, five hundred men walked out of a steel mill while it was still in operation. A Union spokesman said they had to strike while the iron was hot.

323. A hymn has recently been dedicated to a Birmingham corset factory. It is 'All Is Safely Gathered In.'

324. 'In tipped cigarette smoking we may be dragging behind the rest of the world,' said a doctor last night.

325. An M.P. took his seat in the House of Commons today – but he was forced to put it back.

326. A few hours ago two chairmen of rival oil-stove manufacturing companies were involved in a heated argument.

327. In his bid to become an M.P., Mr. John Berkeley-Wilson-Hepplewhite, has applied for re-election to the human race.

328. On Saturday a fair will be held at the small village of Rotting Green. Most of the visitors will be undertakers so the organizers confidently hope it will be a fete worse than death.

329. A dry cleaner was excused jury service yesterday because he claimed his business was very pressing.

330. Three tons of human hair to be made into wigs was stolen today from East Grinstead. Police are combing the area.

331. It was announced today that British Rail are to place boards over the bottom of the lavatory doors at Waterloo Station. A spokesman said this was to prevent limbo dancers from getting in free.

332. Yesterday evening saw the opening of a new play starring that famous actress noted for her snake-like movements, Anna Conder. Her remarkable performance moved many people – to go and visit the bar.

333. A compass has recently complained of going round in circles.

334. Last night an amazing hush fell on the audience at the opening of the new play: 'Nurse Anna Stetic – the thing with the lamp.' It was little William Hush, who had fallen from the balcony.

335. The B.B.C. are to spend £500,000 next year on radio programmes for the deaf.

336. As from midnight on Thursday, under a new pay award, barbers are to get fringe benefits.

337. It was the coldest day in Britain yesterday for the past twenty years. At Brighton three mechanics were sitting in a garage, shivering, when they heard a knock at the door. On opening the door, the wind howled past them and they saw a shaking, shivering monkey who looked up and said: 'Excuse me, do you do welding?'

338. Several small frauds have come to light since accountants moved in at the building firm of Smash, Smash & Build. The new owners of the Company are to employ hordes of people from Czechoslovakia and a number of tight rope

walkers to supervise the accounts. It will be a system of Czechs and balancers.

339. A man was trapped on the roof of a blazing block of flats this evening. He escaped by taking all his clothes off, looking at the astonished audience below, and walking down the stares.

340. A carpet said to a floor today: 'O.K. Don't move I've got you covered.'

341. Not to mention the all-metal noticeboard which commented this morning: 'You can't pin anything on me.'

342. A Scotsman was fined for indecent conduct at Edinburgh on Friday. According to witnesses the man had continually wiped the perspiration off his forehead with his kilt.

343. In a speech last night the Prime Minister, in replying to questions, said it was not true that old people were living from hand to mouth – it was just that they had to do without the luxuries of life – such as television, housing, clothing, food . . .

344. Late last night a large hole was made in the walls surrounding Sunnyview Nudist Camp at Bigglehampton. Police are looking into it.

345. The police are also looking for a man with one eye. Typical inefficiency!

346. A lady dropped her handbag over the edge of a railway platform this morning. The porters refused to retrieve the handbag as they considered it beneath their station.

347. A man jumped into a 482 mile long river in France in the early hours of this morning. He was said to be in Seine.

348. I have just shot some very strange animals that were chewing my typewriter. That is the end of the gnus.

349. Little Puddlington's Arts Festival this year is to include a revolutionary new play in which all the characters remain clothed throughout the entire evening. The audience, however, is expected to strip instead.

350. It was officially announced today that, due to the ever-increasing use of Hyde Park by dogs, the area is now to be designated as a huge open cess pit and play area for dogs. Humans will now be banned from the Park, announced the new mayor, Mr. Woof – who, incidentally, is believed to be a small basset hound and only this country's second canine mayor since dogs were given the vote. The first non-human mayor was, of course, the well known Miss Growl of Hove who has represented the town for several years.

351. Mrs. Blackhorse has sent a petition of three names to the Prime Minister complaining about the recent comedy programme which included scenes of men wearing trousers. Said Mrs. Blackhorse: 'I think it is disgraceful! Since at least the year 1980 men have gone without trousers in favour of kilts and it is now the accepted and proper custom to do so. To show men wearing such ancient and sexually provocative clothing – particularly that sensuous Harris Tweed suit – is morally corrupting to the nation's youth.' Mrs. Blackhorse is $5\frac{1}{2}$.

352. A further two girls are to be admitted to Prankton College – the former all-male public school. The first two girls – sent to the school a couple of years ago – are said to be somewhat exhausted and so need replacements. They were not replaced sooner because the boys have only just discovered that the two girls were slightly different from boys – they tired more quickly when playing rugby.

353. It was announced today that the New Forest is to be turned into a museum – although the Forest at present only consists of two trees, six blades of grass, a small pony, three

hundred chemical toilets, three hundred thousand tons of rubbish and one and a half stuffed deer.

354. Mrs. Bloggs-Smith was fined six thousand pounds on Thursday for talking in a public place at a rate of 95 decibels – five decibels above the permitted level. Although she explained she had to talk at this level to make herself heard above the noise of the Hippo Jets at the nearby airport, she was still ordered to also undergo an operation to reduce the risk of such offences occurring again.

NOSE

355. My young son took his nose apart this morning. He wanted to see what made it run.

NUNS

356. Two nuns were out for a drive in the country and the nun at the wheel of the car was also busily knitting.

Two policemen, seeing this, chased after the car in their patrol vehicle. Drawing level with the nuns' car, a policeman shouted from his window: 'Pull over.'

'No it's not,' shouted back one of the nuns, 'it's a woolly cover for a hassock.'

357. Inscription on a nun's tombstone: 'Returned – unopened.'

358. 'Why is Sister Mary getting so fat? I thought she was on a diet?'

'She is. But it's a seafood diet. She sees food and eats it.'

359. Not to mention the nun with a forty-six inch bust who couldn't get a bra big enough so went, weeping, to Mother Superior saying: 'My cup runneth over.'

NURSING

360. Anna Stetic – the nurse who was a real knockout.

361. Young girl: 'I'd like to see a sturgeon.'

Nurse: 'Don't you mean a surgeon?'

Young girl: 'Well, I want a contamination.'

Nurse: 'An examination?'

Young girl: 'Yes, that's right. I think I'll have to go to the fraternity ward.'

Nurse: 'Fraternity ward? Oh, you mean maternity ward, I think.'

Young girl: 'All I know is I haven't demonstrated for two months and I think I'm stagnant.'

362. Patient: 'Give me a kiss, nurse.'

Nurse: 'No.'

Patient: 'Please give me a kiss, nurse.'

Nurse: 'Certainly not!'

Patient: 'Go on, nurse, kiss me!'

Nurse: 'No, sir – and I'm not even supposed to be in bed with you.'

363. Pretty young nurse: 'Doctor, every time I take this young man's pulse it gets much faster. Should I give him a sedative or something?'

Doctor: 'No. Just give him a blindfold.'

364. 'Nurse, is it true that uncooked eels are healthy?'

'I imagine so, sir. I've never heard any complaining.'

365. 'Give it to me straight, nurse, how long have I got?'

'It's very difficult to say, sir. But if I were you I wouldn't start reading any serials.'

366. Handsome young man, from behind a screen: 'I've taken all my clothes off, nurse. Where shall I put them?'

Young nurse: 'On top of mine.'

O

OCTOPUS
367. Just before Christmas Fred tried to cross an octopus with a chicken – so his family could have a leg each.

ORCHESTRA
368. The orchestra had just finished playing a delightful little number called 'Tuning Up', and the audience were eagerly awaiting the arrival of the world-famous conductor, Igor Driftwood.

The tension mounted as the brilliant conductor delayed his entrance until the last possible moment – then he appeared and the audience went wild with delight, clapping and jumping up and down in ecstasy at being so privileged to see such a man of sheer genius.

Igor made his way to the conductor's platform to even greater cheers. He tapped his music stand, and all was silence.

Then he looked down at the music stand and said: 'Er ... excuse me, but what are these five lines with all the black dots and funny squiggles on them?'

ORPHANAGE
369. When asked for a donation to the local orphanage a Scotsman sent two orphans.

OWLS
370. When it is very stormy and pouring with rain owls are not very keen to go romancing. All they do is sit in the trees looking very dejected – hence their call: 'Too wet to woo; too wet to woo.'

P

PAINTING

371. Artist: 'You know, you're the first model I've ever made love to.'

Nude model: 'I don't believe you. I bet you say that to all the models you've painted. How many have you had?'

Artist: 'Well, there was a bowl of fruit, a dog, the water-mill ...'

PARROT

372. Mrs. Green had a truly remarkable parrot and when the vicar came to tea one afternoon she could not resist demonstrating to him how clever her pet was.

'If you pull this little string on its left leg Polly will sing "Abide With me",' said Mrs. Green, proudly. 'And if you pull the string on its right leg it will sing "Onward Christian Soldiers".'

'How remarkable!' exclaimed the vicar. 'And what happens if you pull both strings at once?'

'Simple!' replied the parrot. 'I fall off my perch, you stupid old twit.'

373. For three years Amy Clegg's parrot had not said a single word, and eventually she became convinced it was simply a stupid parrot unable to learn to speak English.

Then one day as she was feeding it a piece of lettuce as a special treat, the parrot suddenly squawked: 'There's a maggot on it; there's a maggot on it!'

Amy Clegg was astonished. 'You can talk!' she exclaimed. 'But why haven't you spoken in all the three years that I've been keeping you?'

'Oh,' replied the parrot, 'the food has been excellent up to now.'

374. Fred at last could see a way of making a fortune. He had trained his parrot, after months of hard work, to tell jokes.

At last he felt ready to cash in on all his hard work, so he took the parrot down to his local pub.

'This is my incredible joke telling parrot,' boasted Fred.

'Go on,' jeered the pub regulars. 'We'll give you ten to one that your parrot can't tell us a joke.'

'All right,' replied Fred. 'I accept your bet.'

But try as he could, Fred was unable to make the parrot talk – let alone tell jokes.

Fred left the pub, dismally, having lost the bet. On the way home he shook the parrot and shouted: 'What do you mean by keeping quiet, you stupid bird? You made me lose a ten to one bet!'

'Ah!' squawked the parrot. 'Tomorrow you'll be able to get fifty to one.'

PENICILLIN
375. Penicillin – the present for the man who has every-thing.

PERSONAL LIFE
376. My father was very religious – he wouldn't work if there was a Sunday in the week.

377. I used to be engaged to a contortionist – until she broke it off.

378. In dangerous situations I always keep a cool head – usually on the top shelf of the larder.

379. I always carry some olive oil around with me in case I ever meet an olive that needs oiling.

380. You know, beneath my father's hard, cold exterior – there's a hard, cold heart.

381. I was an unwanted child – my mother wanted puppies.

382. Our family was so poor my sister was made in Hong Kong.

383. I've always believed in love at first sight – ever since I looked into a mirror.

384. I was born with a silver spoon in my mouth. Once it was taken out I was all right.

385. I love kids. I used to go to school with them.

386. My father was very kind. When it was cold he used to throw an electric fire into my bath.

387 And my mother believed in germ free food. She even put arsenic in my sandwiches to kill them.

388. No, that isn't my own moustache I'm wearing – my real one is in my pocket.

389. I don't smoke, don't drink and don't make passes at my girlfriend – I make my own dresses, too!

390. I learned to swim at a very early age. When I was three my parents used to row me out to sea in a little boat until they got about a mile or so away from the shore – then I had to swim back. I quite liked the swim – it was getting out of the sack that was difficult.

PIANO
391. What do you get when you drop a grand piano down a coal mine? A flat miner.

392. 'I heard you were moving your piano so I came to help.'
   'Thanks, but I got it upstairs already.'
   'Did you do it alone?'
   'No, I hitched the cat to it.'
   'How on earth could a small cat haul a grand piano up three flights of stairs?'
   'Used a whip.'

POACHER
393. 'So! Caught you at last,' hissed the gamekeeper, emerging from the bushes behind a poacher.

'What do you mean?' asked the poacher.

'I saw you hastily throw that plucked duck back into the river as soon as you saw me. Look, there it is – still floating on the surface. And how do you explain all its feathers on your clothes?'

'Simple! The duck wanted to go for a swim so I'm minding its clothes.'

POLICE

394. What did the policeman say to the man with three heads?

' 'Allo, 'allo, 'allo.'

395. She was only a police constable's daughter, but she let the chief inspector.

396. Policeman: 'Anything you say may be taken down . . .'
Man: 'Knickers!'

397. The car was racing along the motorway at well over a hundred miles per hour when it was forced to stop by a police car.

'You were exceeding the speed limit, sir,' said a policeman. 'Would you mind blowing into this breathalyser to see if you are fit to continue your journey?'

'But I'm in a great hurry,' replied the middle-aged male driver. 'I'm perfectly fit to drive. Can't you just give me a speeding ticket and let me continue on my journey? My wife and six year old daughter are desperately trying to get to a party on time.'

'I'm afraid I must insist on you blowing into the breathalyser, sir,' persisted the policeman.

'But I'm perfectly capable of driving,' said the man. 'Look, try out your breathalyser on my young daughter – the thing may not even be working properly.'

The policeman agreed to this suggestion and the man's six year old daughter blew into the breathalyser. To the policeman's surprise, the breathalyser turned green. He admitted to the man that it must be faulty, so hurriedly wrote out a speeding ticket and let the man continue on his journey.

'I told you it would be a good idea,' said the man to his wife after they travelled a few miles.

'Yes,' agreed his wife. 'Giving our daughter a glass of rum before we set out was one of the best ideas you've had yet.'

398. 'Is that the police?' asked a panic-stricken voice on the 'phone to the police headquarters.

'Yes, this is the police station,' replied the officer on duty.

'Oh, thank goodness! I want to report a burglar trapped in an old lady's bedroom. Please come quickly!'

'Who is that calling?' asked the policeman.

'The burglar,' replied the voice on the 'phone.

399. The body of a man was found today in Hyde Park. The body had been hacked into a thousand pieces and tied in a sack. Police do not yet know if it was suicide.

400. 'Hello! Is that the police station?'

'Yes.'

'Have any lunatics escaped near here recently?'

'Not that I know of, sir.'

'Oh!'

'Why do you ask?'

'Someone's run off with my wife.'

401. Policeman: 'Anything you say may be held against you.'

Writer: 'Samantha Fox.'

POLITICIANS

402. It is no use telling politicians to go to hell – they are trying to build it for us now.

403. A lifelong Socialist was lying, dying, on his bed when he suddenly decided to join the Tory party.

'But why?' asked his puzzled friends. 'You've been a staunch Socialist all your life.'

'Well, said the dying man, 'I'd rather it was one of them that died instead of a Socialist.'

404. A man went for a brain transplant and was offered the choice of two brains – an architect's for £100 and a politician's for £10,000.

'Does that mean the politician's brain is much better than the architect's?' asked the man.

'Not exactly,' replied the brain transplant salesman, 'the politician's has never been used.'

POP MUSIC

405. The new record, 'Nitrogen', is a gas.

406. The pop group threw a stick of dynamite into the audience. That really brought the house down.

407. Interviewer: 'Can you read music?'
Pop star: 'No. I can only read four letter words.'

408. 'Can I sing my little number now?'
'Yes.'
'Three!'

409. Interviewer: 'Do you feel you have any obligations towards your fans?'
Pop star: 'Yes. Particularly the ones that have taken out paternity suits against me.'

410. Interviewer: 'What are those tiny bongoes dangling from your ears?'
Pop star: 'Oh, they're just me ear drums.'

411. Interviewer: 'Can you play any musical instrument?'
Pop star: 'Yes. I'm very good on the barrel organ.'

412. Interviewer: I hear you have just played the Stradivarius?'
Pop star: 'Yes. That vile inn down the road.'

POPULATION EXPLOSION
413. The only reason there is a population explosion is because it is such great fun to light the fuse.

PORCUPINES
414. How do porcupines make love? Carefully ... very carefully.

PORNOGRAPHY
415. Timothy Tittle, a rather shy middle-aged man, got lost in the back streets of Soho one day.

Suddenly a furtive looking man in a shabby raincoat slipped out of a shop doorway and sidled up to Timothy.

'Want to buy any pornographic pictures?' asked the man.

'Certainly not!' replied Timothy. 'I don't even own a pornograph.'

PROFESSOR
416. A country yokel and a professor were in a train, and as it was a long journey they eventually got to talking.

'Every time you miss a riddle you give me a pound, and every time I miss one I give you a pound,' said the professor, when they had run out of the usual things to talk about.

'Ah, but you're better educated than me, so I'll give you 50p and you can give me a quid,' suggested the yokel.

The professor agreed and the yokel made up the first riddle: 'What has three legs walking and two legs flying?'

The professor didn't know, so he gave the yokel a pound. The yokel didn't know either, so he gave the professor 50p.

417. A professor dedicated his whole life to research on insects and their behaviour.

Eventually, after many years of patient study, he was ready to announce his findings to the world.

A special meeting of the world's top experts on insects was arranged, and the meeting was thrown open to the press as well – for the professor felt his findings were so amazing that the whole world should be informed.

When the audience were all seated, the professor strode into the room, ready to reveal the result of his researches.

The professor placed a spider on a table in front him and commanded the spider to walk three paces forwards. To the astonishment of the audience, the spider did as it was ordered.

'Now take three paces backwards,' commanded the professor. Again, the spider obeyed the command.

Then the professor pulled all the legs off the spider, put it back on the table and said: 'Walk forward three paces.' The spider did not move. 'Walk forward three paces,' commanded the professor, again. But still the spider did not move.

'You see,' said the professor, proudly, 'that proves that when you pull its legs off it can't hear.'

PROTESTER'S PLACARDS
418. 'SAVE WATER – BATH WITH A FRIEND.'

419. 'SAVE SPACE – BREED SMALLER PEOPLE.'

420. 'NO ARMS FOR VENUS DE MILO.'

PSYCHIATRIST
421. 'I'm worried. I keep thinking I'm a pair of curtains.'
   'Stop worrying, and pull yourself together.'

422. Then there was the psychiatrist who woke up one day to find himself under his bed. He decided he was a little potty.

423. 'I keep wanting to paint myself all over with gold paint.'
   'Oh! You've just got a gilt complex.'

QUACK DOCTOR

424. 'Roll up! Roll up! Buy this miraculous cure for old age and colds. Rigor mortis can be cured! Roll up! Roll up!' called the fairground quack doctor.

He soon collected a large crowd around his stall, and the quack went on to proclaim the merits of his products. 'This miraculous mixture actually cures old age. You have only to look at me to see the proof of its power. I am over two hundred and fifty years old.'

One astonished man in the crowd turned to the quack's beautiful young assistant and said: 'Say, Miss, is what the gentleman says really true? Is he really over two hundred and fifty years old?'

'I'm afraid I can't really say,' replied the quack's assistant. 'I've only been working for him for the past ninety-three years.'

QUESTIONS

425. Does fishing result in net profits?

426. If a plug would not fit, would you socket?

427. Is a drunken ghost a methylated spirit?

428. Do manufacturers of rope have all their assets tied up?

429. If an artist becomes angry does he lose his tempera?

430. Is the Privy Seal a creature with flippers kept in a privy?

431. After 1902 was Rhodesia a difficult country to travel in because there was no Rhodes?

432. Is a budget a baby budgerigar?

433. If you sat in a bucket of glue would you have a sticky end?

434. Is playing tennis courting disaster – or is it a racket?'

435. 'What is fire?'
'That is a burning question.'

436. 'Write on one of the following: Sir Thomas More, Tudor furniture, Hampton Court.'
'No thank you. I prefer to write on paper.'

437. Say what you know about the French Revolution.'
'Nothing.'

438. 'Write in your own words – such as fghytu, trwdbv, liuthg, lkhteb, jkhbvod . . .'

439. What is the difference between a buffalo and a bison? Ever tried to wash your hands in a buffalo?'

440. What goes up bell ropes and is wrapped in a polythene bag? The lunchpack of Notre Dame.

441. What is soft, sings, and cleans windows? Shammy Davis Jnr.

442. What is sticky and used to sing? Gluey Armstrong.

443. If you suddenly heard a tap on the door would you immediately suspect a mad plumber?

444. What's afoot? The thing connected to your ankle.

445. What's afoot? Twelve inches.

446. How do you defeat someone? Chop off everything above their ankles.

447. What is hairy and coughs? A coconut with a cold.

448. What is smooth, round and green and conquered the world? Alexander the Grape!

449. What is the difference between unlawful and illegal? Unlawful is against the law. Illegal is a sick bird.

450. What is the opposite of minimum? Minidad.

451. What is brown and sounds like a bell? Dung!

452. What is one of the main causes of sleepwalking? Twin beds.

453. If a buttercup is yellow, what colour is a hiccup? Burple.

454. What does a Hindu? Lay eggs.

455. How do you stop moles digging in the garden? Hide all the shovels.

456. What are hippies for? To hang your leggies on.

457. Why do birds fly south in winter? Because it's too far to walk.

458. What is yellow and very dangerous? Shark infested custard.

459. What has got twelve legs, one eye and four tails? Three blind mice and half a kipper.

460. What has got four legs and flies? A dead horse.

461. What is it when a jester carries a nun? Virgin on the ridiculous.

462. What do you get if a cat swallows a ball of wool? Mittens.

463. Is the Eiffel Tower the ultimate in Gallic symbols?

464. What is the difference between a barrow boy and a dachshund? The barrow boy bawls his wares on the pavement – and the other . . . has blue eyes.

465. What was the campaign slogan of ancient lizards millions of years ago? Things will be better come the evolution.

466. What weighs two tons and wears a flower behind its ear? A hippy potamus.

467. What has an I.Q. of 144? A gross of Irishmen.

468. What goes in dry, comes out wet and pleases two people? A tea bag.

469. Did the coroner who lost his pub go on an inn quest?

470. What lies at the bottom of the sea and shivers? A nervous wreck.

471. Where do you find mangoes? With womangoes.

472. Why does a giraffe have such a long neck? Because it can't stand the smell of its feet.

473. What do you put on a pig with a sore nose? Oinkment.

R

RABBIT
474. As the exhausted American rabbit said: 'Gee, I'll never do that for ten bucks again!'

RACING
475. The very expensive racehorse continually lost races which everyone had expected it to win.

'Perhaps what it needs is a bit more encouragement,' suggested the horse's owner.

So the jockey warned the horse just before the start of a major race that if it lost the race it would be the end of its racing days and the horse would have to find work elsewhere – probably on a milk round in the country.

The horse nodded at the jockey to indicate that it understood this threat, and soon the race began.

Unfortunately, this horse was soon trailing behind all the others and as the jockey urged it forward with his whip the horse turned its head and said: 'Steady on, sir. I've got to be up early in the morning.'

476. 'Are you sure you're a qualified jockey? You've put the saddle on the wrong way round.'

'How do you know which direction I'm going in?'

477. 'Why is the horse trainer in hospital?'

'Well, he was boasting about how good he was – that he could train any four-legged creature to win any race and he'd even win riding it without a saddle. So someone gave him a porcupine . . .'

RATS
478. Two rats were in a large glass container into which tobacco smoke was being passed as a laboratory experiment. One rat coughed to the other: 'I wouldn't mind so much if they cut us in on the coupons.'

RED CORPUSCLES
479. The two red corpuscles – they loved in vein.

REINCARNATION
480. I've believed in reincarnation ever since I was a young frog.

RHINOCEROS
481. 'And I shall call that creature a rhinoceros,' said Adam, pointing to a rhinoceros.

'But why call it that?' asked Eve.

'Because,' snapped Adam, 'it looks like a rhinoceros – that's why, stupid!'

ROMANCE
482. My girlfriend says there are things a girl shouldn't do before 20. I'm not too keen on an audience, either.

483. Pretty young girl: 'If I go up to your room do you promise to be good?'

Young man: 'Why – I promise to be FANTASTIC!'

484. Her boyfriend only had one fault. He had Tarzan eyes – they swung from limb to limb

485. My brother was badly beaten up recently fighting for his girlfriend's honour. She wanted to keep it.

486. She started licking my cheek tenderly. I said: 'Do you love me?' She said: 'No – but I need the salt.'

487. My sister had to give up her last boyfriend because he was tall, dark, and hands . . .

488. Two young girls were talking in their office canteen when the subject, as usual, came round to discussing the men in their office.

'I wouldn't have anything to do with Graham Smith, if I were you,' said one of the girls.

'But why not?' asked her friend. 'He seems such a nice sort of man.'

'Ah! But he knows an awful lot of very dirty songs.'

'But surely he doesn't sing them in the office?' asked the friend. 'I've never heard him singing dirty songs.'

'No, perhaps not – but he certainly whistles them!'

489. 'Will you marry me?' asked the young man, getting down on his knees and offering the girl a glittering ring.

'Oooooh!' exclaimed the girl, 'are they real diamonds.'

'I hope so,' said the young man. 'Because if they aren't I've been swindled out of a pound.'

490. The young girl arrived home late from an evening out with her boyfriend. As she stomped into her flat and slammed the door her flatmate came out of her bedroom to see what all the noise was about.

'Oh!' exclaimed the girl. 'Berkeley really is the limit! I had to slap his face several times this evening!'

'Why, what did he do?' asked her flatmate, eagerly.

'Nothing, unfortunately,' muttered the pretty young girl. 'I had to slap his face to see if he was awake.'

491. Young man, turning to the young girl seated next to him: 'You know, Joan,' he said, 'your parents have invited me over to dinner so often I'm beginning to feel sort of obligated. Will you marry me?'

492. 'Say when, dear.'

'After the drinks, darling.'

493. A young girl was entertaining a rather amorous boyfriend at her home late one evening. 'If you kiss me again,' she warned, 'I'll have to call a member of my family.'

Her boyfriend kissed her passionately.

'Bro-ther,' she murmured.

494. 'If I refuse to go to bed with you, will you *really* commit suicide?'

'That has been my usual procedure, yes.'

495. There's nothing so restful as the sleep of the just – except, perhaps, the sleep of the just after.

496. 'Darling, I want to make love before we get married,' said the girl, snuggling up to her boyfriend.

'But it won't be long until July, dear,' he replied.

'Oh!' she exclaimed enthusiastically, 'and how long will it be then?'

497. He used to go out with a girl called Ruth. Then she left him, so he became ruthless.

498. When I met my boyfriend we were both rough and ready. He was rough – I was ready.

499. When we were courting we sat in the fridge because she said she wanted to slip into something cool.

500. Contraceptives should be used on every conceivable occasion. (Spike Milligan)

501. Give me your heart, darling – I'm making a monster.

502. 'Darling, what do you think of the Middle East position?'

'I don't know, I've never tried it.'

503. I met Claudia Hott-Iron yesterday – she made a great impression on me.

504. Man, snuggling up to girl: 'Am I the first man you ever made love to?'

Girl, pushing man back and looking at him carefully: 'You might be – your face looks familiar.'

505. It's hard to keep a good girl down – but lots of fun trying.

506. The man kissed the girl passionately.

Girl: 'I thought a quick one before dinner meant a drink.'

507. 'He loves you terribly.'

'I keep telling *him* that.'

508. There's nothing like a mink coat to thaw a cold shoulder.

509. 'Darling, whisper something soft and gooey in my ear.'

'Lemon meringue pie.'

510. 'James, take off my dress. Now my bra, and now my panties . . . and if I ever catch you wearing my clothes again I'll smash your stupid face in.'

511. So I lay this beautiful young girl on the grass, ripped off her dress, tore off her stockings, grabbed hold of her panties . . . and tore out the elastic for my catapult.

S

SADIST

512. Masochist: 'Hit me!'
Sadist: 'No.'

513. Then there was the sadist who thought his wife looked horrible in stripes – so he stopped whipping her.

SALVATION ARMY

514. 'Hello! Is that the Salvation Army?'
'Yes, it is.'
'Is it true that you save fallen girls?'
'Yes.'
'Then will you save one for me for Thursday night?'

SCHOOL

515. A small boy, absent from school for two days, returns.

'Hello, Barry,' said his teacher. 'Why have you been away from school?'

'Sorry, miss, my dad got burnt.'

'Oh!' said the teacher, 'nothing serious, I hope.'

'They don't mess about at the Crematorium, miss!'

516. Teacher: 'I'll give this shiny apple to anyone who can tell me who was the greatest man in the world.'

Little David Cohen put his hand up and said: 'It was Jesus, miss.'

Teacher: 'Well done, David – you're perfectly right. But I always thought you were Jewish?'

David: 'So I am, miss. And *you* know and *I* know it was really Moses who was the greatest man in the world – but business is business.'

517. 'What are you making, Tommy?' asked the woodwork teacher.

'A portable,' replied the small boy.

'A portable what?'

'I don't yet know, sir. I've only made the handle.'

518. 'Mummy, teacher was asking me today if I have any brothers and sisters who will be coming to school.'

'That's nice of her to take such an interest, dear. What did she say when you told her you are an only child?'

'She just said: "Thank goodness!"'

519. Pupil: 'Can I have a cigarette?'

Teacher: 'Good heavens! No, certainly not! Do you want to get me into trouble?'

Pupil: 'Well, all right then, Miss. But I'd rather have a cigarette.'

520. A little boy and a little girl were walking home from school.

'Guess what I found behind the radiator in our class?' asked the little boy.

'What?' inquired the little girl.

'I found a contraceptive behind the radiator.'

'What's a radiator?'

521. Chemistry teacher: 'What can you tell me about nitrates?'

Pupil: 'Well sir ... er ... they're a lot dearer than day-rates.'

522. A middle-aged woman was on her way to the shops when she saw a small boy leaning against a wall, smoking a cigar and swigging a bottle of whisky. The woman was appalled at this and rushed over to the boy and demanded: 'Why aren't you at school at this time of day?'

'At school?' queried the boy, taking another swig at the bottle. 'Hell, lady, I'm only four years old!

523. A teacher warned her pupils to wrap up warm against the cold winter, and to show how important this was she told them of the true story of her little brother who took his

sledge out in the snow one day. Unfortunately, her brother hadn't been wrapped up properly and he caught pneumonia and died a few days later.

There was silence in the classroom for a few moments, than a small voice at the back said: 'Please Miss, what happened to his sledge?'

SCHOOL REPORT

524. Music: Has a very musical ear, which gives B flat when twisted.

525. English: Knott upp two hiz bezt werk. Iz badd att speling annd mayks litle efort.

526. Science: I am enclosing the bill for one science laboratory.

527. Mathematics: 3 and easy, but 2 easily distracted 4 various reasons.

528. Religious Knowledge: He will definitely go to Hell.

529. History: He likes dates – and figs. Knows much about the Cabinet – much to their horror.

SCOTTISH

530. It was a Scottish wedding – the confetti was on elastic.

531. The meanest Scotsman in the world was the one who fired a revolver on Christmas Eve outside the door, then came in and told his children that Father Christmas had committed suicide.

532. Not to mention the Scotsman who broke in next door to gas himself.

533. A scotsman was travelling across the Forth Bridge when he was asked for his ticket. After searching himself without success he told the ticket inspector he must have lost his ticket.

The inspector did not believe this, so he questioned the

Scotsman further, but the Scot insisted on sticking to his story.

Eventually, the inspector lost his temper and threw the Scot's large suitcase over the bridge.

'Hoots, mon!' complained the Scot. 'First ye try to make me pay twice, and then ya droon ma wee boy!'

SEA
534. Young man: 'Sir, your daughter was struggling in the sea so I pulled her out and resuscitated her.'

Retired colonel: 'Then, by George, you'll marry her!'

SÉANCE
535. The little girl was taken by her father to a séance which was being held at the home of a friend of his who worked in the same factory.

When they arrived at the house the séance had just started and the medium asked the little girl if there was anyone she would like to speak to. 'I'd very much like to talk to my old grandmother,' replied the little girl in a soft voice.

'Certainly, my dear,' said the medium, and shortly afterwards went into a trance. Suddenly the medium began to talk in a strange voice – the voice saying: 'This is your old grandmother speaking from Heaven – a glorious place high in the skies. Would you like to ask me anything, my child?'

'Yes, grandmother,' said the little girl. 'Why are you speaking from Heaven when you're not even dead yet?'

SERVANTS
536. The mother of one of the servants came storming into the lord's manor, demanding to see the lord.

'What is it you want?' asked the lord, when the angry woman was brought before him.

'It's about my daughter, Jenny – she works here,' said the woman. 'You've got her pregnant!'

'Don't worry,' replied the lord. 'If she really *is* pregnant then I'll give you ten thousand pounds – and when the little one comes along I'll set up a trust fund for thirty thousand pounds. Does that seem fair?'

'You're very kind,' agreed the woman, 'but if it doesn't happen – will you give her another chance?'

537. The lady was having an argument with her maid. Before leaving the room the maid decided to say exactly what she thought.

'You might like to know,' she said, 'that your husband told me only last week that I am a far better housekeeper and cook than you are. He also said I was much better looking!'

The lady remained silent.

'And that's not all,' continued the maid, 'I'm far better than you in bed.'

'I suppose my husband told you that as well!' snapped the lady.

'No,' replied the maid, 'the gardener did.'

SEX

538. Blessed are the pure – for they shall inhibit the Earth.

539. In the East End of London people learn about life very quickly.

Two boys were playing in the street when they saw a friend peering through a window into a house.

'Quick!' he said. 'There's a man and a woman fighting in bed.'

One of the other boys, aged about six, looked and said: 'They're not fighting – they're making love.'

The third little boy had a look, too, and said: 'Yes – and badly.'

540. Brian's mother and father had told him about the facts

of life, but when it came to telling their younger son, only seven years old, they were too embarrassed.

'Brian, will you tell John about the birds and the bees?' pleaded Brian's father.

Brian agreed and that night Brian asked John: 'Do you know what mum and dad do at night in bed?'

'Of course I know,' replied John.

'Well,' said Brian, 'it's the same with birds and bees.'

541. How do you tell the sex of a hormone? Take its genes off.

542. Today all the young girls are out all night sowing their wild oats – and in the morning you can find them praying for a crop failure.

543. A gamekeeper was walking across a clearing when he saw a nude young woman walking towards him.

'Are you game?' he asked.

'Yes,' she replied.

So he shot her.

SHIPWRECKED SAILOR

544. A shipwrecked sailor had been drifting about on a raft for weeks, when one day he suddenly sighted land. As he came closer to the shore he saw a group of people on the beach building a gallows.

'Thank God!' cried the shipwrecked sailor. 'A Christian country!'

SHOES

545. 'This pair of shoes you sold me last week is ridiculous! One of them has a heel at least two inches shorter than the other. What do you expect me to do?'

'Limp.'

SIN

546. The wages of sin are high – unless you know someone who'll do it for free.

547. During a conversation with a kindly old priest, the young man asked: 'Is it really such a sin to sleep with a girl?'

'Oh no,' replied the priest, 'but you young men – you don't sleep.'

548. 'Now, what have we got to do before we can get forgiveness of sin?'

'Sin.'

SPEECHES

549. The rather conceited politician was giving his usual long, boring, speech – when one of his suffering audience could stand it no longer.

As a bullet whistled past the speaker's ear, the conceited speaker said: 'I see my speech is so moving that a man in the front row was moved to commit suicide. Unfortunately, he needs an optician as the bullet just missed my ear.'

550. A business executive had to make a speech at an important meeting attended by his business associates. He couldn't think of anything interesting to talk about, so in the end he decided to talk about sex.

When he arrived home his wife asked him how his speech had gone. He replied that it had been a huge success.

'But what did you talk about?'

The man thought for a few seconds, then replied: 'Oh, sailing.'

The following week one of the man's business colleagues approached the man's wife at a cocktail party and commented: 'That was a marvellous speech your husband made last week.'

'I know,' replied the wife. 'It's amazing. He's only tried it twice. The first time his hat blew off and the second time he was sea-sick.'

SPIES

551. Boris Goronovitch, the Russian sportsman and top

secret agent, arrived in Swansea. His highly secret assignment was to contact Jones at the address he had been given. But the address turned out to be a large block of flats, in which five men, all named Jones, happened to live.

Taking a chance, Boris Goronovitch knocked on the door of the Jones on the first floor. As the door opened, Boris whispered: 'The wombats are migrating early this year.'

'Oh, no!' came a voice from within. 'I'm Jones the Milk, the local milkman. You want Jones the Spy – two floors up. Good-bye!'

552. A British diplomat in Moscow was attending a dinner party at the Kremlin, and much to his enjoyment he found himself seated next to a beautiful young woman.

During the course of the meal the diplomat dropped his handkerchief, and gently stroked the ankle of the young woman as he picked it up. But this brought no response.

The diplomat soon dropped a fork, and gently patted the woman's knee when he picked up the fork. But the woman still remained silent.

As he dropped his knife to the floor, the diplomat noticed the young woman scribbling hastily on the back of a menu. She handed him what she had written and the diplomat was somewhat surprised to read: 'When you reach your destination show no astonishment. Roger Barrington-Smythe, M.I.5.'

SUIT
553. I've just bought a suit that fits me like a glove – four trouser legs and one sleeve.

SUNDAY SCHOOL
554. The Sunday School teacher was talking to her class of ten year olds when she suddenly asked: 'Now, why do you think the Children of Israel made a Golden Calf?'

The children were silent until one spotty little boy put up

his hand and said: 'Please Miss, perhaps, it was because they didn't have enough gold to make a cow.'

555. Yet another Sunday School teacher asked one of her pupils if he could say who it was that sat at God's right hand.

Little Jimmy paused, then hazarded a guess: 'Mrs. God, do you think?'

SURVEYS
556. 'Excuse me, madam, we are doing a survey. Can you tell me what you think of sex on the television?'

'Very uncomfortable.'

SWISS
557. How do you make a Swiss roll? Push him off the top of an alp.

T

TAXATION
558. The income tax authorities have now produced a new, simple tax form with only two sections: (a) How much do you earn?; (b) send it.

559. The tax inspector received an income tax return from a bachelor executive claiming a dependent son. He thought this was rather odd, so he sent back the form with a note stating: 'This must be a typist's error.'

Back came the form from the executive, together with a pencilled marginal comment next to the inspector's, saying: 'You're telling me.'

TELEPHONE
560. Bell invented the telephone, but he found it was useless until he invented the second telephone. This was fine, until he invented the third telephone, 'phoned the second, and found it engaged.

THROAT
561. The man cleared his throat – by taking out his tonsils, tongue and teeth.

TIGER
562. Then there was the tiger who caught measles and became so spotty the other tigers banished him to the leopard colony.

TOAST
563. Modern technology is wonderful! In the bad old days we always used to burn the toast every breakfast time – now we can buy the latest automatic toaster and the burnt toast pops up automatically.

TRAFFIC LIGHTS
564. What did the traffic lights say to the sports car? Don't look now, I'm changing.

TRAVEL
565. 'How long is the next bus?'
   'Oh, about eighteen feet.'

566. It was the first scheduled passenger flight to the Moon. The two hundred passengers fastened their seat belts and the gigantic spaceship nosed its way up through the clouds towards its far off destination.

The passengers could hear the soft throbbing of the powerful engines and settled back in their comfortably padded seats to enjoy the journey.

Then a voice broke in on the passengers and said: 'Good morning, ladies and gentleman! And a very warm welcome to Mini-Moon Trips – and our first scheduled passenger flight to the Moon. It may interest you to know that this brilliantly constructed spaceship has been checked and double checked; and to eliminate the possibility of any human errors the spaceship is completely crewed by robots; so rest assured, ladies and gentlemen, nothing at all can go wrong . . . can go wrong . . . can go wrong . . .'

567. While travelling in a sleeping compartment in a train, the man in the top bunk was woken up by someone tapping from below. 'Hello?' he said.

'Are you awake?' asked a female voice from below.

'Yes.'

'It's terribly cold down here. I wonder if you would mind letting me have an extra blanket.'

'I've got a better idea,' replied the man. 'Let's pretend we are married.'

'That's a lovely idea!' giggled the woman.

'Right,' said the man, 'now get your own damn blanket!'

568. A middle-aged woman clambered on to a London bus with three sets of twins trailing behind her. When they were all seated in the bus, the conductor asked her: 'Do you always get twins?'

'Oh, no!' replied the woman. 'Hundreds of times we don't get anything.'

569. Bernard was on holiday abroad and decided to visit the local bazaar.

'Want to buy the genuine skull of Moses?' asked a stall owner.

'Not really,' replied Bernard. 'It's much too expensive.'

'What about this skull,' said the stall-owner, producing another skull. 'This is much cheaper, because it's smaller – the skull of Moses as a child.'

570. As the train thundered along, the man turned to the woman in the otherwise deserted compartment and said: 'Would you let me kiss you for fifty pence?'

'Certainly not!' retorted the woman.

The man returned to his newspaper.

A few minutes later, the man asked: 'Would you let me kiss you for a thousand pounds?'

'Yes,' replied the woman, after a brief pause.

A few minutes later the man asked: 'Would you let me kiss you for a pound?'

'Certainly not!' exclaimed the woman. 'What kind of a woman do you think I am?'

'We've already established that. Now we're just haggling over the price.'

571. If a broad bean is a double-decker bus and a runner bean is a single-decker bus – then what is a pea? A relief.

572. 'Does this train stop at Charing Cross?'

'Well, there will be a right old smash if it doesn't.'

UNITED STATES OF AMERICA

573. A man on holiday in the U.S.A. was amazed at the way his host, a huge Texan, had everything so much larger than back home in England.

The car was as long as three English cars put together; the bedrooms were big enough to play a tennis match in; and the kitchen was so big it could cook enough to feed an Army.

The Englishman was very impressed with all this Texan greatness, but after he had been staying in his host's gigantic house for about a week he began to drink even more than he normally did back in England.

One night, after getting particularly drunk, the Englishman fell into his host's swimming pool. When the servants rushed to rescue him they found him screaming: 'Don't flush it! Don't flush it!'

574. It was on a sightseeing coach tour of New York that the Welshman turned to his companion, a boastful American, and said: 'And where do you come from?'

'From God's own country,' replied the American.

'Hmm,' said the Welshman, 'then you've got a very poor Welsh accent!'

575. We're continually hearing about the terrible crime rate in America, but is it true?

For example, when I arrived in New York a few months ago, a man sidled up to me and said: 'Want to buy a watch?'

'How much?' I asked.

'Sssh!' said the man, 'the guy next to you is still wearing it.'

UNIVERSITY LIFE

576. The appointment has been made of Mr. Otomoto Un-

tumbo to the University language department. He will be teaching Swahili on Mondays, Thursdays and Fridays. On Tuesdays and Wednesdays the students will be teaching him English.

577. The University lecturer was speaking to an audience of townspeople. He was attempting to prove there was a definite connection between happiness and the amount of sex in people's lives.

To help prove his point, he asked those in the audience who indulged every night to raise their right hands. Only five per cent did so, all laughing merrily.

He then asked how many indulged about once per week, and seventy percent raised their hands, smiling contentedly as they did so.

Then the people who indulged once very month were asked to raise their hands, but it was noticeable that these people neither laughed nor smiled.

The lecturer felt that this proved his point – but to show how obvious this matter was, he asked those who only indulged once every year to raise their hands. A tall man at the back of the hall leapt from his chair, waving his hand and laughing loudly.

The lecturer was astonished at this apparent contradiction to his lecture, and he asked the man if he could explain why he was so happy.

The man replied: 'Certainly. It's tonight! It's tonight!'

578. A don was delivering a lecture about the various ways of making love. He began: 'There are fifty ways of making love . . .'

'Eighty-two,' came a voice from the back.

The don, used to such interruptions at this University, decided to ignore the interruption, and continued: 'There are fifty ways of . . .'

'Eighty-two!'

'Be quiet!' rapped the don, his patience at an end. 'I am

trying to deliver an important lecture.' He began again:
'There are fifty ways of . . .'

Voice from back: 'Eighty-three!'

579. The rumour that Mr. Pitt, the new University lecturer,
is an escaped convict has been officially denied. Mr. Pitt has,
in fact, served his sentence.

580. Lecturer to rowdy audience: 'I will not begin until this
room settles down.'

Student: 'Go home and sleep it off!'

581. The female student went to the end of term ball taking
two handkerchiefs with her, as she had a cold. One handkerchief she put in her handbag and the other she tucked down
the front of her dress.

During the course of the evening she finished using the
first and so tried to retrieve the second, but she couldn't find
it.

The University's Chancellor, sitting nearby and watching
her with interest, was amazed to hear her remark: 'I could
have sworn I had two when I came in.'

582. One female student to another: 'The new tutor is gor-
geous, isn't he. He dresses so well.'

Second girl: 'Yes, and so quickly, too!'

V

VAMPIRE
583. The sun-scorched vampire was crawling through the desert, crying 'Blood! Blood!'

VAN GOGH
584. Did Van Gogh cut off his ear because he was only half ear?

585. Van Gogh: 'My dear, please take this ear as a token of my affection for you.'
Woman: 'Th . . . thank you.'
Van Gogh: 'Pardon?'

VET
586. 'Martha!' shouted frail little Sidney from his bed. 'I'm terribly sick, please call me a vet.'

'A vet?' queried Martha. 'Why do you want a vet and not a doctor?'

'Because,' replied Sidney, 'I work like a horse, live like a dog, and have to sleep with a silly cow!'

VICARS
587. A vicar called Mark was closing the Church doors after an evening service when he heard a strange voice call: 'Mark! Mark!'

He looked outside the Church, but could find no one calling his name. Then he looked inside the Church, but although the voice still called 'Mark! Mark!' the poor clergyman could not find where the sounds were coming from.

Finally, he rushed to the altar, thinking it must be God calling him. But when he got there all he found was a dog with a hare lip.

588. One small village in Sussex was so heathen that the inhabitants proved too much for all the clerymen sent to look after the local church. In fact, they got rid of so many vicars it might be said they had 33⅓rd revs. per minute.

589. A very attractive young girl was about to enter the Church in a topless dress when the vicar ran towards her.

'I'm very sorry, madam,' said the vicar, 'but I cannot possibly allow you to go into Church like that.'

'But I have a divine right,' protested the young girl.

'Yes,' agreed the vicar, 'and you have a divine left, too, but I still cannot let you into my Church like that.'

590. The vicar was passing the local pond when he heard a little voice. He looked around, but could see no one. But the voice continued. Then he saw a frog sitting near the edge of the pond. The frog told the vicar that it had been turned into a frog by a wicked witch. The vicar was naturally horrified and asked the frog what he could do to help. The frog said that he was really a ten year old boy and all the vicar had to do to remove the witch's spell was to take him home and put him in the vicar's nice warm bed. And that, m'lud, concludes the evidence for the defence.

591. The vicar was explaining the difference between knowledge and faith to his congregation.

'In the front row,' he said, 'we have Mr. Heather with his wife and three children. Now, she knows they are her children – that's knowledge. He believes they are his children – that's faith.'

592. Vicar: 'You know, I pray for you every night.'

Young woman: 'Well, there's really no need – I *am* on the 'phone.'

WAR
593. During the War he was in France when they fired the first shot ... he was in Australia when they fired the second.

WATCH
594. 'What does your watch say?'
  'Tick, tock!'

595. You know my rustproof, elephant proof, shockproof, waterproof watch? Well, it's just caught fire.

WATER SKIER
596. An Irishman bought a pair of water skis – now he spends all his time looking for water with a slope.

WEDDING
597. I once knew a very sporting country gentleman who put a silencer on his shotgun because he wanted his daughter to have a quiet wedding.

WHALES
598. Where do you weigh whales? At a whale weigh station.

WIDOWS
599. A man is dragging a large box along the pavement when he suddenly stops outside one house and knocks at the door.
  The door is opened by a woman, and the man asks: 'Are you Widow Jones?'
  'My name is not Widow Jones,' replies the woman, 'It's Mrs. Jones.'

'Wait till you see what I've got in this box,' says the man, sorrowfully.

600. One of Henry's best friends had died, so shortly after the funeral he called on the widow in order to express his sympathy.

'John and I were very good friends,' he said. 'Is there something I could have as a small memento of him?'

The widow raised her tear-stained eyes and looked at Henry. 'How would I do?' she asked, hopefully.

WILL

601. The solicitor was reading Humphrey's will and had just come to the last paragraph. 'I always said I'd mention my dear wife, Joan, in my will,' read out the solicitor. 'So, hello there, Joan!'

WISHES

602. A little old lady was busy making herself some tea one afternoon when a fairy appeared in her kitchen.

'You've led a long and good life,' said the fairy, 'so I've come to reward you and tell you that you can make three wishes. Ask for absolutely anything you like and with one wave of my magic wand, you can have it.'

The old lady found this very difficult to believe, so she asked the fairy to turn the teapot into a pile of pound notes. The fairy waved her magic wand and the teapot promptly turned into a pile of money.

'My!' exclaimed the old lady. 'It really does work! Now, can you make me look young and beautiful?'

The fairy waved her wand again and in a few seconds the little old lady was transformed into someone looking young and beautiful.

'And now I'd like you to turn my dear old cat into a handsome young man.'

This, too, was soon done, and the fairy left the old-but-now-young-and-beautiful-looking-lady alone in her kitchen with the handsome young man who had formerly been a cat.

The lady turned to the man and sighed: 'At last! Now I want to make love to you for the rest of the day and night!'

The man looked at her, then said, in a very high pitched voice: 'Then you shouldn't have taken me to the vet's, should you?'

WORMS
603. Then there were the two worms in the graveyard making love in dead Ernest.

WRESTLING
604. I've got nothing against watching professional wrestling – I just wish I had a low enough I.Q. to enjoy it.

WRITER
605. The best selling writer was being interviewed about his career.

'It seemed to me, after fifteen years of full-time writing, that I was absolutely hopeless and had no talent at all for writing.'

'So what did you do?' asked the interviewer. 'Decide to give up writing?'

'Oh, no!' replied the writer. 'By that time I was far too famous.'

X

X-RAY

606. The medical lecturer in the newly opened Medical School turned to one of his pupils and said: 'Now, Jones, it is clear from this X-Ray I am holding up that one of this patient's legs is shorter than the other. This of course, accounts for the patient's limp. But what would *you* do in a case like this?'

Jones thought for a few seconds, then said, brightly: 'I should imagine, sir, that I would limp, too.'

XANADU

607. The people of Xanadu are very kind to tourists – they kill them painlessly.

608. The men of Xanadu are probably the strongest in the world. When a fifteen ton lorry is stuck in the mud it is nothing to see one of them walk up behind it and, with one mighty heave, break a shoulder.

609. In Xanadu they've all got great hairy arms and legs; they all smoke massive cigars and have big black moustaches – and the men are just as bad.

Y

YIDDISH
610. David Cohen repeatedly won the great international company's annual award for being the best exports salesman.

After winning the award for fifteen years in succession, having netted his company many millions of pounds worth of overseas business, David was asked how he had managed such a remarkable achievement – especially as he refused to take an interpreter on his journeys abroad.

'It's really quite simple,' explained David. 'At each trade exhibition I just look for a well-dressed man waving his arms about and then I go up to him and we do all our business and so on in Yiddish.'

YORKSHIRE
611. The old Yorkshire farmer was passing through the town one day when he decided to pay a visit to the doctor.

'I should be most grateful,' said the farmer, 'if you would call in one day and take a look at my wife.'

'Certainly,' replied the doctor. 'Is your dear wife ill?'

'I don't really know,' said the Yorkshire farmer. 'But yesterday morning she got out of bed at the usual time of four o'clock in the morning and milked the cows and made breakfast for me and the farmhands; then did the farm accounts; made the dinner; churned the milk; fed the chickens; ploughed a few fields; then made the supper before repainting the living-room – but about midnight she was complaining she was a bit tired. I think, doctor, she needs a bit of a tonic or something.'

YUGOSLAV
612. One Yugoslav woman who was expecting her sixth child was horrified to read in the newspaper that every sixth person born in the world is Chinese.

Z

ZEBRA CROSSING

613. Policeman to jay walking pedestrian: 'Here! Why are you crossing the road in this dangerous spot – can't you see there's a zebra crossing only fifty yards away?'

Pedestrian: 'Well, I hope it's having better luck than I am.'

ZOO

614. The little boy had just returned home after an outing with his father.

'Well, dear, how did you like the zoo?' asked the boy's mother.

'Oh, it was great!' replied the boy. 'And Dad liked it too – especially when one of the animals came racing home at thirty to one.'

ZUB ZUB

615. What goes 'zub, zub?' A bee flying backwards.

OUR PUBLISHING POLICY

HOW WE CHOOSE

Our policy is to consider every deserving manuscript and we can give
special editorial help where an author is an authority on his subject but
an inexperienced writer. We are rigorously selective in the choice of
books we publish. We set the highest standards of editorial quality and
accuracy. This means that a *Paperfront* is easy to understand and
delightful to read. Where illustrations are necessary to convey points of
detail, these are drawn up by a subject specialist artist from our panel.

HOW WE KEEP PRICES LOW

We aim for the big seller. This enables us to order enormous print runs
and achieve the lowest price for you. Unfortunately, this means that you
will not find in the *Paperfront* list any titles on obscure subjects of
minority interest only. These could not be printed in large enough
quantities to be sold for the low price at which we offer this series. We
sell almost all our *Paperfronts* at the same unit price. This saves a lot of
fiddling about in our clerical departments and helps us to give you
world-beating value. Under this system, the longer titles are offered at a
price which we believe to be unmatched by any publisher in the world.

OUR DISTRIBUTION SYSTEM

Because of the competitive price, and the rapid turnover, *Paperfronts* are
possibly the most profitable line a bookseller can handle. They are
stocked by the best bookshops all over the world. It may be that your
bookseller has run out of stock of a particular title. If so, he can order
more from us at any time—we have a fine reputation for "same day"
despatch, and we supply any order, however small (even a single copy),
to any bookseller who has an account with us. We prefer you to buy from
your bookseller, as this reminds him of the strong underlying public
demand for *Paperfronts*. Members of the public who live in remote
places, or who are housebound, or whose local bookseller is unco-
operative, can order direct from us by post.

FREE

If you would like an up-to-date list of all paperfront titles currently
available, send a stamped self-addressed envelope to
ELLIOT RIGHT WAY BOOKS, BRIGHTON RD.,
LOWER KINGSWOOD, SURREY, U.K.